NAVIGATING
LIFE
book 2

Resources, Direction & Answers for Adoption,
ADD/ADHD, Autism, Special Needs,
Parenting Concerns, How to Find Help
and more...

NAVIGATING
LIFE

When and How to Involve a Professional

CRAIG T. MITCHELL, LCSW

NAVIGATING LIFE: Resources:Resources, Direction & Answers forAdoption, ADD/ADHD, Autism, Special Needs, Parenting Concerns, How to Find Help and more....
by Craig T. Mitchell, LCSW
©2019 Craig T. Mitchell, LCSW

All rights reserved. The use of any or part of this publication, whether reproduced, transmitted in any form or by any means, electronic, mechanical, photocopying, recording, or otherwise, or stored in a retrieval system without the prior consent of the publisher, is an infringement of copyright law and is forbidden.

All information and opinions in this book are those of Craig T. Mitchell and do not necessarily reflect the opinion or view of Inky's Nest Publishing.

Edited by Mylynn Felt, Joan Williams and Natalia Burdett
Cover design by Dan Pitts of Dan Pitts Design
danpitts.com
Interior book design by Russell Elkins of Inky's Nest Design

ISBN: 978-1-950741-01-4

Published by Inky's Nest Publishing

1st edition
First printed in 2019 in the United States of America

CONTENTS

1 Adoption **9**

2 ADD and ADHD **19**

3 Autism **35**

4 Parenting and Concerns with Children **41**

5 Delayed Development in Children **67**

6 Identifying Normal and Delayed Development in Children **73**

7 Children with Special Health Care Needs **87**

8 Individualized Education Programs and 504 Accommodations **93**

9 Siblings of Children with Special Needs **109**

10 What Are Our Attitudes about Family Problems and Special Needs **115**

11 Organizations and Foundations for Rare Disorders **119**

12 Be Careful When Researching and Applying Diagnostic Symptoms to Your Family Member **121**

13 Some Suggestions When You Have a Child with a Special Need **123**

14 Respite Care **129**

15 Some Suggestions When There Seems to be Little or No Help **137**

16 Transition Planning for Children with Special Needs **145**

17 Medical Providers and Insurance Companies **149**

18 Choosing a Primary Care Physician or Medical Provider **155**

19 Medical Specialists List and Definitions **163**

Acknowledgments

I would like to thank many individuals who have been instrumental in shaping the direction I have taken in this life. First, I would like to thank my family. My parents provided an example of hard work. They were always there to back me up when I needed support, and they also provided no small amount of help in the form of more hard work on my behalf. My wife, Arlette, was instrumental in teaching me about loving everyone, especially those with special needs. She was truly a Saint who advocated for and took these individuals into our home to give their families needed rest from around the clock care. She was loved by those she cared for and their families. She was also a great mother and disciplined our seven children with tough love when it was needed. My children grew up loving each other and were very patient to accept the other children who came into our home on a regular basis. I am so proud of the contributions they are all making to this world.

One of my high school teachers, James Dorigatti, was instrumental in leading me into my profession as a therapist. The most prominent teachers in my life are Dr. Gary Carson, a psychology professor from college, and JoAnn Larson from graduate school. I can't put in words the inspiration these two people have been to me. I have tried, unsuccessfully, to emulate their professionalism and want them to know how much they influenced my career choices.

I want to thank my patients who over the years have been the reason I love to do therapy. I have always tried to be the best therapist I could for them. I know for some I was not a good fit, just as all doctors or products are not the best for everyone. In these cases, I tried to send them to others who might be better for them. I have learned everything from them and thank them for trusting me to help them get to a better place in life.

I thank my friends who have been there for me, from high school to today. I thank Mylynn Felt, my first editor, Joanie Williams for her input and editing, and Natalia Burdett who was my final editor. I also thank Stephanie Stockdale for her encouragement and prodding during the past several years. I need pushing and she provided it. I am grateful for Russell Elkins and Dan Pitts for their professional guidance and professionalism. I thank Matt Anderson for his work on the ilustrations. Most of all I am grateful for the constant prompting from the creator of us all and the blessings of having such a variety of professional and life experiences, which I believe prepared me to write these books.

chapter one
ADOPTION

Infertility

In the majority of cases where couples consider adoption it is because of a problem with infertility. There are couples who do not have infertility and pursue adoption because of a desire to provide children with a family. To cover this subject I will start with infertility, which is the inability to either become pregnant or to keep a pregnancy through to birth. This can be a very difficult and significant loss to work through for those individuals who are affected by it.

I recall the first time I had an encounter with a couple who was dealing with infertility. I had been working in adoptions for about a year, and I was conducting the required interviews with them. Each time we met it became more obvious to me that this prospective adoptive mother was angry, and I became the object of her animosity. This woman was almost 40 years old which meant that she had less than a year to adopt because 40 was the cut off line in terms of age requirements for the agency I was employed by. I was a bit confrontive because I had become weary of her passive aggressive comments as she was, in essence, blaming me for all of the red tape and time it took to get through the process of adoption. She was obviously anxious that she would be able to adopt a child before she turned 40. I told her that I understood she was impatient and frustrated with the steps we were taking; however, I had no way of making the process shorter. I was part of the mechanism to achieve her goal of being a mother, and we had requirements to complete. I was only the messenger, and I had to execute all the necessary interviews and paperwork the law mandated. I emphasized that we were a team and my goal was to help her qualify for adoption. I remember saying, "Don't shoot the messenger; I am on your team and I am rooting for you." It was remarkable what happened to her when she finally got that baby in her arms. She melted into a very relaxed and pleasant mother. I didn't realize until that time what infertility really was. It carries with it a great sense of loss and its own type of grief. In some cultures, there is stigma and shame associated with infertility.

Studies show that one in four to five couples has difficulty with infertility. The woman who suffers from this problem can have all kinds of feelings. In the early stages, she has anxiety each month hoping to miss having a period and then after many months of disappointment she dreads this time of month because in her mind it is associated with failure. There are also those who have irregular periods or no periods at all. These are just a few of the many problems associated with infertility. Comments from friends and family are all done without understanding how harmful and insensitive they can be regarding having children. Some of these comments are "When are you going to start a family?" "Why are you putting off having children?" or "We are sure looking forward to a grandchild," etc. Just going to a store and seeing all the babies and very young mothers or pregnant women can be painful and a reminder of the deeply felt heartbreak of infertility. Seeing all the teenagers who are pregnant and don't want to be is also very difficult and can cause resentment and anger to build to the point that depression and anxiety become part of a woman's world. This can also be the case if the infertility is because of the man. Eventually, there comes the time, after years of these feelings, when consideration of other options begins to surface. Infertility treatment, with all the tests and attempts to conceive, becomes the routine. If it works, great; but if it doesn't there can be further feelings of failure and hopelessness. Finally, there comes a time for most couples that adoption begins to come into view. Questions are asked of people who have adopted and, step by step, if an adoption plan is accepted the method of which route to take is researched.

Before going on to the different kinds of adoption, I would like to encourage you to look at the chapter in Book 1 on GRIEF and consider the steps you may go through as you grapple with infertility. I also believe you would greatly benefit from reading one of the many books on infertility that are available out there. Doing a search on the internet, browsing in bookstores, and looking at the chapter titles can be insightful in choosing a book that seems to speak to your needs. In some areas there are infertility support groups, and many adoption agencies have such groups or someone who works with couples experiencing infertility. They should know where to refer someone for these groups, and some hospitals have infertility support groups as well. I think you will be surprised as you look closely into these matters at how many others share the same concerns. You are not alone.

Home Studies

Adoption requires that a home study be done to determine if an individual or couple qualifies to adopt. Depending on the type of adoption, the study needs to be done by a licensed social worker or the equivalent such as a psychologist or someone with a degree in a related field, based on local laws. A private adoption can normally be done by a licensed social worker where private adoptions are allowed by law. When an adoption through an agency is being sought, one of their social workers completes the study unless the adoptive applicant lives in another town or state. In such cases, a private social worker or another adoption agency will need to prepare the home study depending on the requirements of what is called the placing agency or the agency who is doing the adoption.

A home study generally requires a social worker or the equivalent to visit the adoptive applicant's home and assess if it meets local standards for adoption. Other individual and joint interviews are also required. Criminal background checks, child abuse checks, letters of employment verification, birth certificates, marriage certificates, medical exams on all members of the family, financial records, tax records, income statements, proof of medical insurance, and a questionnaire regarding many aspects of the applicant's life are all part of the home study process. Listed above are some of the basic requirements of home studies; however, requirements vary in different states and countries.

Some states or agencies require training as part of the home study process. This is very important to prepare the adoptive applicants for the many challenges they may face. Training is required to adopt internationally and when applying for foster care.

TYPES OF ADOPTION

Private

Domestic adoptions are those done within your own country. There are two kinds of domestic adoptions: private and agency adoptions. A private adoption is when a birth parents decide to place their baby for adoption with people they know or she may go to an attorney and enquire if he or she knows of a couple who would like to adopt. The details of terminating the parental rights and finalizing the adoption are usually handled by an attorney. Most states allow this to happen; however, there are a handful of states that do not, and they require every adoption to be done by an adoption agency.

Agency

Agency adoptions are those done by an adoption agency licensed by the state or country where they have offices. Because they are licensed they must qualify for licensure based on the adoption laws established in their jurisdiction. There must be offices with staff to take care of the required work and records on each client must be kept according to policies and procedures established by law. These agencies are monitored by officials who have to visit and make sure all requirements are met to prevent illegal practices. In most states there has to be a master's degree social worker on the staff to maintain the license because their degree prepares them to deal with what are called licensed services. Licensed services refers to foster care and adoption. Most agencies will have foster homes to house an adoptive child for a period of time until the parental rights can be relinquished and the child placed legally. Some agencies are engaged in doing fost/adopt which is the process of placing a child with a family who is licensed for foster care and/or adoption until a decision is made by the proper authorities to either return the child or children to their parents or to terminate their parental rights and place them for adoption with the foster parents. Some agencies offer foster care, adoption, and fost/adopt, meaning the family becomes a foster home first with the hope of adopting a child placed in their home, while other agencies may only offer one or two of these options.

Not always, but on occasion, it can be difficult to terminate parental rights because a birth father might want to parent the child, and the birth mother may be opposed to this happening. This can take months or longer in some isolated cases. Most agencies are very good at dealing with these issues, and they can answer any questions you have regarding these matters. If you are contemplating adoption, I encourage you search for licensed agencies and to ask all the questions you have until you find an agency you are comfortable with.

Foreign/International

Foreign or international adoptions are, of course, adoptions from other countries. In 2008 the United States became a signatory to The Hague Convention. This is an organization that created guidelines for international adoptions to prevent child trafficking, fraud, and other inappropriate adoption practices. The State Department has the responsibility to regulate these adoptions. An organization to accredit or authorize international adoption agencies was identified to make sure they have the necessary Hague requirements in place to conduct foreign adoptions. Agencies who do not work with Hague countries are not required to be accredited.

Agencies have to be licensed by each foreign country where they conduct adoptions. It is a difficult process for agencies to obtain licensure in any foreign country. Countries who allow adoptions have their own requirements which can vary dramatically, even if they have signed on as Hague Convention countries. Some countries have not joined with The Hague Convention and still conduct adoptions. There are more safeguards in place with a Hague country, but there are countries that do a very good job with adoption, and they may never join The Hague Convention because it is expensive and requires that they make many changes to their current systems. People who are looking into international adoption can find a wealth of information on the subject at the U.S. Department of State website, http://adoption.state.gov. This site will give you information on the adoption process, as well as agencies in your state. It will also list which countries are involved in adoption and which ones are Hague compliant and much more. It would be wise to contact an agency and inquire about the process and any other questions you have. If you want to adopt from a specific country, there may not be an agency in your state licensed to do so. In this case you will have to identify an agency licensed to do adoptions in your preferred country. You will need an international home study from a licensed agency in your state that is able to do international home studies. An international home study is vastly different from a domestic home study and will need to be done by an agency experienced in international adoption. In some cases, you will only be able to have a home study done by an accredited Hague Convention agency.

Differences Between International and Domestic Adoptions

Some people prefer domestic adoption because they don't have to worry about children who have been in orphanages or foster care systems abroad. They want to adopt a child with a well-known family background and prenatal history. They may want to have contact with the birth parents, and it is okay in their minds to have an open adoption. They don't want to travel and deal with gathering all the documentation for an international adoption. On the other hand, some do not want the possibility of having an adoption reversed and the child placed back with the birth parents, which has happened in rare but highly publicized cases. This can be avoided with an international adoption.

Post placement/adoption reports completed after the child is in the adoptive home are required in literally all adoptions. In most cases the reports are completed by the agency social worker who did the home study. These reports are usually done in the home of the adoptive parents to assess the development of the child, bonding of the child to the parents and vice versa, as well as any perceived concerns. There are two types of these reports: post placement reports and post adoption reports. Post placement reports are compulsory in the case of domestic adoptions and in some foreign adoptions where the adoption is not finalized in country prior to bringing the child home. These reports are submitted to the adoption agency if it is an agency adoption or to the attorney in a private adoption. These reports are submitted to the court with the home study upon finalization of the adoption. States and adoption agencies generally require one to three post placement reports before finalizing an adoption, and foreign countries can require more depending on the country from which the child was adopted. Post adoption reports are required with all Hague country adoptions and, depending on the country, they might require as few as three over the first year to several during the first two years and then one a year until the child is 18 years old. Most often these reports are completed by the agency social worker for the first year or two and then the rest are done by the adoptive family. They are submitted to the agency who forwards them on to the country where the child was adopted from.

There are many reasons why people choose domestic or international adoptions. Most foreign adoptions are finalized in the country of origin, and there is no chance of the birth parents changing their minds because the child must be an orphan. This gives a security that some need when they adopt. The idea of providing a child from another country with a home that the child otherwise might not have, is compelling to adoptive parents. When adopting a child internationally, some countries require one or both adoptive parents to travel to the country sometimes multiple times. With international adoptions getting a child is assured; the only thing in question is the time it takes. Children who have been in orphanages are at risk for abuse, malnutrition, developmental delays, reactive attachment disorder, undiagnosed medical problems and more. Usually, the longer a child is in an orphanage the more they are at risk for these concerns. However, depending on the child and his or her environment there may be few problems. There are some countries which place children in foster homes instead of orphanages or use a combination of both.

Birth Parents

Those who have children out of wedlock have some real challenges. Deciding what to do can be life changing, and they need all the support they can get. Hopefully, anyone in this situation will have family who can offer love and understanding. It is always good to talk with someone who is objective and is trained to assist someone in this situation. I always recommend that birthparents go to an adoption agency because they are there to discuss all options without pressure. By law they are not supposed to push or influence birthparents to make any choices for themselves and their child. If they chose to keep the child, they are hopefully counseled and referred to appropriate resources for their needs. If they choose to make a plan for an adoption, they are helped through the process. There are many concerns a birth mother may face including fear of the birth father if he is abusive or if she does not want to marry or have contact with him. Often the birth father does not want anything to do with the responsibility of the child or the financial or other responsibilities involved; he just wants complete avoidance. In other situations, birth fathers use the pregnancy to control the birth mother by threatening to take the child. Of course there are situations where the birth father is caring and responsible and wants to be part of the child's life even if adoption becomes the plan. Paternal grandparents may want to raise the child or the birth father may want that opportunity. This puts birth mothers in a precarious position and may change what her decision will be. Obviously, the best scenario is when both birth parents work together regarding the best plan for themselves and the child.

Where to live and what to do during the pregnancy as well as pressure from family or others are all common problems adoption agencies are experienced in dealing with. Uncertainty is always something birthparents experience, and planning one's future is something that can be done with experienced professionals at an adoption agency. Just It may have adoption agency in the title, but realize that they are there to help no matter what the birthparent decides to do. I have worked with birthparents for many years, and these are some of the bravest and most unselfish people I have ever met.

If you are a birthparent and need help, I admonish you to find a list of agencies and do some shopping. You are probably frightened and worried, and the kind and understanding professionals found at an adoption agency may be just what you need. There will be a greater opportunity for counseling and support before and after the adoption with an agency than in a private adoption. There are some attorneys who make efforts to help the birth parents with counseling and most states require a minimum number of hours of counseling to be offered to birth parents. It is important to realize that most birth mothers will need support, in many instances for a life time, to deal with the issues that can arise over the years. This is especially true when birth parents and adoptees are reunited. That is another subject I wish I had space in this book to deal with. To all birth parents, especially birth mothers I wish you the best as you make courageous decisions for you and your child, which will have far reaching consequences.

chapter two
ADD AND ADHD

A number of years ago I began to perform ADHD evaluations. I have seen many children over the years at the clinic where I have been employed for well over 20 years. During this time I have consulted with parents regarding what they can do to better understand and best help their children who have been diagnosed with ADD/ADHD. I have shared with them the information I have gleaned over the years and what studies have revealed. I want to share with you these same ideas. I will be talking to you, the reader of this book, as if you were such a parent. It is very interesting that many of the parents I work with have many of the same behaviors as their children because this condition is hereditary.

What is ADD/ADHD?

ADD is Attention Deficit Disorder. Actually, this diagnosis is technically referred to as Attention Deficit Hyperactive Disorder without Hyperactivity. To qualify for this diagnosis both children and adults must have six of nine symptoms which are from a list found in the DSM-IV and the newer DSM-V, or the Diagnostic and Statistical Manual for Mental Disorders, published by the American Psychiatric Association. This becomes confusing to many people, which is why many professionals prefer to refer to it as ADD or Attention Deficit

Disorder. There are many organizations who publish symptoms of ADD which are very similar, but they all get their start with the DSM-IV.

These 9 ADD symptoms are all related to inattention:

- Fails to give attention to details or makes careless mistakes in schoolwork or other activities
- Has difficulty sustaining attention to tasks or activities
- Does not seem to listen when spoken to directly
- Does not follow through on instructions and fails to finish schoolwork (not due to oppositional behavior)
- Has difficulty organizing tasks and activities
- Avoids, dislikes, or is reluctant to engage in tasks that require sustained mental effort
- Loses things necessary for tasks or activities (school assignments, pencils, or books)
- Is easily distracted by extraneous stimuli
- Is forgetful in daily activities

You will note here that this diagnosis is made based on these nine symptoms. Many other diagnostic tools in the form of questionnaires have been created, which ask many related questions of parents and teachers to diagnose this condition. However, these questionnaires are all related to the nine basic symptoms.

ADHD is Attention Deficit Hyperactivity Disorder. Usually, this is what is called Combined Type where the child has at least six of the nine symptoms of ADD and then six of nine symptoms related to Hyperactivity and Impulsivity. A child can be diagnosed with Hyperactivity/Impulsivity without Attention Deficit Disorder. This is called ADHD Hyperactive Type.

The following nine symptoms are divided into six hyperactive symptoms and the last three are impulsive symptoms:

- Fidgets with hands or feet or squirms in seat
- Leaves seat when remaining seated is expected
- Runs about or climbs too much when remaining seated is expected
- Has difficulty playing or being quiet during play activities
- Is on the go or often acts as if driven by a motor
- Talks too much
- Blurts out answers before questions have been completed
- Has difficulty waiting his or her turn
- Interrupts or intrudes on other's conversations and or activities

Simply put, there are 18 symptoms of ADD/ADHD and there are three possible diagnoses:

- ADD or Attention Deficit Disorder. This is when the person has at least six of the Inattention symptoms only.
- ADHD Hyperactive Type. This is when the person has at least six of the Hyperactive/Impulsive symptoms only.
- ADHD Combined Type meaning Inattention with Hyperactivity. This is when the person has at least six of the symptoms for both Inattention and Hyperactive/Impulsive types.[1]

---

1   *Desk Reference to the Diagnostic Criteria from DSM-IV.* P. 63-65. 1994 American Psychiatric Association.

Controversy about ADD/ADHD

Over the years, I have heard all the negatives about ADD/ADHD. These vary from, "the medication makes kids zombies," to "the doctors are getting paid by the drug companies." I have also heard, "There is no such thing as ADD/ADHD; the child is just lazy." Some parents believe food coloring and sugar cause their children to be hyper. There are many things said to deter people from considering this as a legitimate diagnosis. There is enough medical and research evidence demonstrating that this is a real disorder.

I have seen situations where medications are prescribed with doses being too high, which can cause the patient to be drowsy and can affect his or her appetite. The most common symptom with these medications is lack of appetite. Some people do not respond to or do well with medication.

Diagnosing ADD/ADHD

When I do an evaluation for ADD/ADHD I always use three different diagnostic tools or questionnaires. There are many such questionnaires which are used for this purpose, and all of them ask the person filling out the form to respond to many questions related to the 18 criteria listed above. If a child is in school, I always want the teachers and parents to fill out the questionnaires as well. This is important because we can get very different responses from the school as opposed to the parents based on the different environments the child experiences. Often a child will do better in school because it is a much more structured environment; however, I do see some children who have fewer symptoms at home. This is why it is important to consider both environments.

In order to diagnose this condition, some people advocate having a psychologist or trained observer going to the child's school and observing the child for a few hours to several days. Realistically, most families don't have the money to pay for a psychologist to do such an evaluation. Just observing a child for an hour or two in an office or at school, one may not see the typical problematic behaviors, especially if the child knows he or she is being watched. I have had many parents say that the behavior of their child in my office is not typical for him or her. Observed behavior can vary from the extreme of being very hyperactive to being very calm and quiet. Observation in an office setting is not the key in diagnosis. There is wisdom in having parents, care givers and teachers fill out the questionnaire because it will paint the most accurate picture of the child's most common behaviors, since they spend the most time with the child. This is why the questionnaires are designed for both the teacher and the parents.

If a Diagnosis Is Made

If, after considering all the information from parents and school, a diagnosis of ADD or ADHD hyperactive type, or ADHD combined type is made, I then discuss with the parents their options from medications to behavioral approaches. We discuss if a doctor or psychiatrist may be needed. Many of these patients are referred by their doctor, and we make sure he or she receives a copy of the evaluation. If the family does not have a primary care doctor, I will discuss a referral to a doctor who is comfortable dealing with ADD/ADHD. We also talk about who their insurance allows them to see. Sometimes it is best for them to go to a child psychiatrist and having insurance is important because they can be expensive and hard to get an appointment in a timely manner.

I always try to encourage the parents to take a parenting class since their parenting skills will be severely challenged with a child who has one of these diagnoses. I refer the family to CHADD (Children and Adults with Attention Deficit/Hyperactivity Disorder) which is a national organization that helps families with information regarding ADD/ADHD. They have local chapters which sponsor support groups and speakers to educate families regarding research, various treatments, and ways of dealing with ADD/ADHD. The website for CHADD is www.chadd.org.

I also explain to the parents regarding information and concepts I learned years ago which still apply today. There is a concept called the reticular activator which is the brain's ability to filter out the extraneous stimuli that bombard all of us each day. For example, in a classroom a light flickers and the child who has ADD/ADHD sees it and looks up to understand what is going on. This child with ADD/ADHD does not have a reticular activator that is filtering. It is like all the volumes on his or her senses are turned up to 10. This includes vision, hearing, and touch. Children without ADD/ADHD do not pay attention to the light because their filtering systems are working. They can read a book, do an assignment, or focus on what the teacher is saying because this filtering system is working. The same applies when a bird flies by the window, or when someone whispers or drops a pencil. The child with ADD/ADHD is unable to ignore the disturbance, albeit a very slight one, because his or her brain is not filtering. Again, students without this ADD/ADHD are able to ignore these distractions because their brains are filtering. When medication is introduced, it enhances the filtering process.

I believe the reason children with ADD/ADHD are very intelligent is because they see, hear, and sense more of what is going on in the environment because their brains are not filtering. This gives them many more opportunities for sensory input and therefore some learning is almost always going on because they are getting so much more information from their surroundings. The problem with this condition is that the child is so overwhelmed with extraneous stimuli that he or she can't follow instructions or process information. For those who do not have ADD/ADHD it is like trying to write a research paper or do math problems at a carnival with all the noise, lights, moving objects and people talking. The commotion cannot be ignored or tuned out.

Books I Recommend for ADD/ADHD

At this point in the evaluation, I recommend to parents and adults two books on ADD/ADHD. There are many other books out there which are excellent on this subject. I don't like to overwhelm people, so I stick with two books that I find have good, practical information.

The first book I recommend is *Healing ADD: The Breakthrough Program That Allows You to See and Heal the 7 Types of ADD* by Daniel Amen, MD. He has identified seven different types of this disorder and has specific strategies parents and professionals can use to treat each one of these types. In his book he has a questionnaire to fill out for the person you think has ADD. After answering the questions, instructions are given to score and identify which type of ADD the person has. Once the ADD/ADHD has been diagnosed one would go to the chapter dealing with that type of ADD and put into use his treatment strategies. There are many other good books on this subject so check ADD Warehouse online.

Causes of ADD/ADHD

Dr. Amen is a psychiatrist who has done extensive brain imaging (PET scans or positron emission tomography) of patients with ADD/ADHD. He has discovered that there is less blood flow in the brains of individuals with ADD/ADHD compared to those who do not have this condition. This leads to fewer nutrients within the brain causing less brain activity. Imaging of patients' brains after taking medication shows normal levels of blood flow and more normal brain activity.

The second book is *A Bird's Eye View of Life with ADD/ADHD* by Chris Zeigler Dendy and Alex Zeigler. I attended a lecture by Dr. Dendy and have been recommending her book for my patients ever since. The following information is from her book:

Between five to 12 percent of the population has ADD/ADHD.

It is a complex neurobiological problem that affects the white matter of the brain. The majority of children who have ADD/ADHD are smart. There is nothing wrong with their grey matter; the problem lies within the white matter or the wiring of the brain.

I believe the following information is probably the most important concept Dr. Dendy made while researching for her book. It has to do with what scientists have discovered regarding the brain in individuals who have ADD and ADHD.

The brain has grey matter and white matter. The grey matter is the computer and the white matter is the wiring. When messages are sent to other parts of the brain the white matter is the path or conduit these electrical impulses travel through. These paths are called neurons and when they get to a certain point in their journey they have to cross a gap between one neuron and another. This gap is called the synapse. To accomplish this, the messages are sent across on tiny particles called neurotransmitters. Just before they jump across to the other side, a signal opens a gate called a receptor on the receiving side of the neuron to accept the neurotransmitter. When this process happens properly the message is transferred to the other neuron and then it continues on in the form of an electrical message. When this step is complete the neurotransmitters are recycled or sent back to the other side of the synapse to the sending neuron, where they started so they can be used again. This describes how a brain without ADD/ADHD functions properly.

This process is different within the brain of someone with ADD/ADHD. The signal that opens the receptors on the receiving side of the neuron does not function properly. When these receptors do not open the neurotransmitter is unable to attach to the other side of the neuron in order for the message to be sent on. When this happens, the neurotransmitters are recycled back to where they started much too quickly or they are absorbed. This makes it easier to understand how people with ADD/ADHD aren't able to process what they are listening to and then don't respond appropriately.

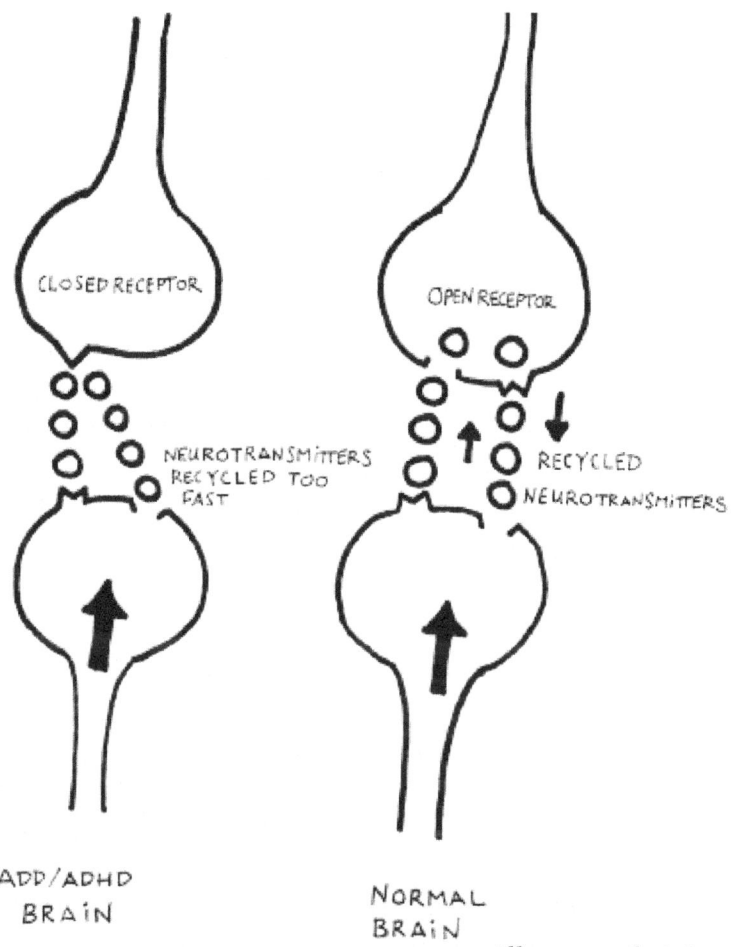

Illustration by Matt Anderson

This is why a parent says to a child, "Please pick up your shoes, please pick up your shoes, please pick up your shoes." Then finally on the fourth time the comment is, "I have now asked you four times to pick up your shoes," and the child says, "No you didn't," "Yes I did and now I am saying it for the fifth time." We now understand what is going on in the brain of someone with ADD/ADHD and I hope this knowledge gives parents a new appreciation for what is not happening in the child's brain when this occurs. This should also give adults with the same diagnosis a better understanding that they are not dumb or abnormal. They have a biochemical condition in the wiring of the brain.

Medication helps the receptors on the receiving side of the neuron to open, allowing the neurotransmitters to be encoded and the message is sent on to where it is supposed to go. The person can listen, focus, and comprehend directions more normally. He or she can finish tasks or homework and are more able to remember to hand in homework and be better organized.

Improvement in behavior is another advantage of medication. Because this is a complex neurobiological problem, medications are more successful in treating the disorder, whereas behavioral approaches do not correct this biochemical condition. Over the years, as I have reviewed many ADHD studies, it has been interesting that medications have always been more successful in treating ADD/ADHD than behavior strategies, and now with this new information we understand why. When studies compare the outcome of treatments for ADD/ADHD they consider medication, behavior modification, and medication with behavior modification. Dr. Dendy has discovered that medication and behavior modification is the best treatment approach, and medication alone comes in as a very close second. Behavior modification is much less effective, used by itself. As I say to the parents I meet with, it is very difficult to teach a young, distracted and hyperactive child to say to himself or herself, "I need to stop and consider the consequences of my behavior and start focusing on my work." It is too difficult for a young child to do this without help in the form of medication to change his or her brain chemistry.

In her presentation, Dr. Dendy played a video of Dr. Ted Mandelkorn who is a pediatrician. As he talks to the parents of his patients, he asks them if they ever walk to another part of their home to do something and then forget why they are there. Of course this is normal for most people. He goes on to indicate that children with ADD/ADHD are doing this all day long. ADD/ADHD is a biochemical problem in the brain. When the child gets medication on board, they are able to choose what to do with their brains and their successes become their choices. Prior to taking medication, their brains were not cooperating, and they were unable to choose to make decisions as do others without this disorder.

Children with ADD/ADHD have slower brain maturation of about 30 percent. Therefore, we need to realize that these children will be less mature and need more supervision and support. Dr. Dendy paraphrases Dr. Russell Barkley who has done extensive work regarding ADD/ADHD. In essence, he said an 18-year-old is more like a 12-year-old. If this student is to be successful, you need to put the supports in place for a 12-year-old in the classroom.

Two-thirds of those with this condition develop coexisting conditions such as learning disabilities, anxiety, depression, oppositional defiant disorder, and substance abuse. They also have difficulty with executive function or organizing various aspects of their life, especially school. It is also inherited in over 50% of the cases. Medication works in 75 to 90% of patients, and this is a lifetime problem that most people will not outgrow.

Some other important facts are that children who consistently take medication for ADHD are less likely to abuse drugs later on because without treatment they begin to self-medicate and look to other substances. Kids with ADD/ADHD have a difficult time going to sleep at night and have a hard time waking up in the morning. There are many other things you should know about these diagnoses, and I encourage you, if you have a child with the symptoms listed above, that you make an appointment with your doctor and purchase Dr. Dendy's book.

My Experience with ADD/ADHD

I, myself, have struggled with ADD all my life. I didn't realize this until I was almost 40 years old. As a student and in college and also in graduate school, I had a very difficult time listening to professors and taking notes at the same time. I could only do one of these tasks at a time. I found myself thinking something was wrong with me because I observed other students all around me having no problem listening and taking notes. I was always asking, "What was that they just said?" I also had problems reading textbooks. I would read a paragraph and could not remember what I had just read. I was always distracted and thinking of other things. Despite this, I found ways to study and get through school.

When my oldest daughter was in college she decided to talk to her doctor about ADD. They decided to try her on medication and the first day she took it she came home very excited and exclaimed that she could now listen to the professor and take notes at the same time. Before this she was just like me and could only do one or the other. This changed the rest of her college life as she was able to focus and stay on task as well as take notes and remember her lectures. After graduating, she was hired immediately into a supervisory position and continued to take medication until her doctor told her she needed to find a local physician to write her prescriptions because she had been living in another city. Because of this she did not take meds for over a year. She finally decided to find a local doctor and now she is back on medication because she does reporting and payroll and finds she is much more efficient when taking her medicine. I have another son and daughter who both take medication for ADD. My son has been taking it for almost 10 years now, and he is much more able to stay on task while on medication. He started taking medication when he was in college also. My other daughter started taking medication after earning her bachelor's degree. She is also more organized and effective when taking her medication.

My Strategies for My Own ADD

I have a number of personal techniques or strategies I use to counter my Attention Deficit Disorder. Whenever I set something down like my cell phone or a tool or whatever, I try in every instance to say to myself THREE times. "I put this right here; I put this right here; I put this right here." When I do this, I remember where it is later, as long as it isn't months later. One of my part-time jobs is doing adoption studies, which is like writing a research paper a couple of times a month. They are usually 10 to 15 pages in length. Many years ago, I started using a speech recognition program where I sit in front of my computer and talk into a microphone, and the program types out the words for me. It is very accurate and has become more so over the years. When I sit down to write, I make sure all my materials are ready to go in one folder. I read and highlight with a bright highlighter/marker all the statements I am going to place in the document. Then I turn on the microphone and read the highlighted statements. I tell myself I am going to go to a certain point and then I take a break. This gives me a goal to reach, in manageable chunks, before my mind starts to wonder. I set these short term goals in all my work and then get my reward in terms of a break with a soft drink or treat or a walk, etc. Sometimes at home, I take a break and putt or chip some golf balls or watch a little TV or read something I want to learn for this brief period of time then I get back at it.

More Interesting Strategies

I had a woman tell me a strategy she uses with her adult son who has ADD. He returned to live with her for a short time, and one evening he stayed out late until early in the morning without telling her. The next morning, she went up to him and said, "Last night you were out until early in the morning; I worried all night and could not sleep. What are you going to do next time?" He said, "I'm sorry I will call and let you know." She said again, "Last night you were out until early in the morning; I worried all night and could not sleep. What are you going to do next time?" He said, "I will let you know Mom." She said again, "Last night you were out until early in the morning; I worried all night and could not sleep. What are you going to do next time?" He said, a little frustrated, I will call and let you know if I will be late! She said the fourth time, "Last night you were out until early in the morning; I worried all night and could not sleep. What are you going to do next time?" He said in a firm voice, "Okay, Mom I get it!" She always does this with him, repeating four times what she needs him to understand until she believes he gets the point.

Another idea that seems to help when waking a child in the morning is to stand at the door until he or she actually gets out of bed. I know this takes extra time, but if you stick with it and decide you are going to do what it takes to get results then it can prevent a lot of frustration going back and forth to the child's room.

What to Do When You Think Your Child has ADD/ADHD

The bottom line here is to make an appointment with your doctor and tell him or her of your concerns. The doctor will be able to either diagnose the condition or send you to the right resource to either rule it out or get a diagnosis regarding what the problem might be. Some primary care doctors are comfortable diagnosing this and some are not. Psychiatrists diagnose this as well as most psychologists and some social workers or other trained professionals. You will find that some primary care doctors and pediatricians will not feel comfortable prescribing medication if your child does qualify for a diagnosis of ADD/ADHD. Therefore, you may need to consult with your doctor regarding who to see you if you want to try medication as a treatment option.

For sure you will need to become adept at handling the difficult behaviors produced by a child with ADD/ADHD, regardless whether or not medication is part of treatment. I always recommend that parents take a parenting class. Please refer to the chapters on PARENTING AND CONCERNS WITH CHILDREN'S BEHAVIOR and A BRIEF EXAMPLE OF A PARENTING COURSE to understand my reasoning. If you can find a children's behavior therapist to help both yourselves as parents and your child, this would be the ideal.

These professionals are child therapists and psychologists, etc. that work with children and parents to incorporate methods of dealing with problematic behaviors within the family. These professionals can be difficult to find so ask around and do an internet search for child behavior therapy and hopefully you will find someone who will work with you and your child. In addition, your child may need some counseling or play therapy for younger children up to about 10 years of age or so. If he or she is mature enough then other methods of counseling might be beneficial. Again, refer to the chapters above for more insights about this subject. There are a number of other types of treatment such as biofeedback, which can be beneficial. Your doctor is a good resource to consult with regarding these other methods of treatment, so go ahead and ask him or her about other treatment resources in your area.

chapter three
AUTISM

Much could be said about autism, but I will try to be brief and get to the main points of this very difficult and puzzling disorder. In recent years autism has taken a brighter stage, so to speak, because it has become so much more diagnosed than in the past. The Center for Disease Control or CDC estimates that 1 in 88 children in the U.S. have an autism spectrum disorder. Individual states report rates from 1 in 210 children to 1 in 47 children.

Autism in the Past

Until 2013, autism was classified under a category called pervasive development disorders. Although there are other disorders under this grouping, three specific types were the most frequently diagnosed, Pervasive Developmental Disorder (PDD), Asperger's Disorder, and Autism Spectrum Disorder. It may sound confusing, but it is important to understand that Pervasive Developmental Disorder and Asperger's Disorder were both considered within the broad definition of autism disorder. For all intents and purposes, autism had essentially taken the place of the major category of PDD, and PDD had taken a place as a condition on the autism spectrum. Autism is described as a spectrum disorder because it can be very mild or very severe based on the number of symptoms a child has. The concept is similar to assessing the extent of hearing loss. With testing it is possible to determine if there is no hearing loss or 0% up to 100% hearing loss if there is no hearing at all. This is how broad the category for autism is, although it is not rated on a scale from 0 to 100, but rather from mild to severe.

Pervasive Developmental Disorder or PDD NOS until 2013

When a child had significant deficits in social interaction, verbal or nonverbal communication, or in persistent and repetitive behaviors without demonstrating the symptoms of a specific type of pervasive developmental disorder, (autism or Asperger's) he or she likely received the diagnosis of Pervasive Developmental Disorder. The exact name of this disorder was Pervasive Developmental Disorder not otherwise specified or PDD NOS. This diagnosis was given to children who had impaired social skills and repetitive behaviors but did not meet the criteria for autism. This may have meant the child's symptoms were less severe than the other diagnoses but not always. It simply meant the child's symptoms didn't fit neatly into a diagnosis under Pervasive Developmental Disorders. As the child grew older he or she might have improved more quickly leading to a retraction of the PDD diagnosis or the symptoms could have become specific enough to justify a diagnosis of Autism Spectrum Disorder or Asperger's.

Asperger's Disorder

The diagnosis of Asperger's was based on a number of symptoms including; impairment of social appropriateness such as nonverbal behaviors like eye contact with others, understanding of facial expressions or body and hand gestures. In addition, the inability to form appropriate social relationships, absence of spontaneous social interaction like sharing enjoyment with others, and gesturing to objects or things of interest including sharing back and forth with others. Also, repetitive behaviors like being fixated on something such as an idea or activity with routines and rituals becoming inflexible. Repetitive body movements and fixation on parts of objects was the other aspect of this disorder. These symptoms are found in the DSM-IV referred to in this book which is now replaced by the DSM-5 with a new method of assessing autism. With the publication of the new DSM-5, PDD and Asperger's are no longer considered diagnoses. There is just one major category of Autism Spectrum Disorder. I will explain this shortly.

Diagnosing Autism

Finding someone to diagnose autism can be difficult depending on where you live. Schools do not normally diagnose autism; however, I have seen some do it in a few cases over the years. Some child psychiatrists and developmental pediatricians who specialize in autism will diagnose this disorder, but, most commonly, child psychologists are those who do evaluations for autism. The highest regarded method for evaluating autism is a system called ADOS or the Autism Diagnosis Observation Schedule which takes a minimum of two to three hours or much more to complete. Again, this is usually done by psychologists who are trained in testing procedures. This includes an interview to record history and then a testing session. Some psychologists will evaluate a child based on interviews and possibly questionnaires completed by parents and teachers without using the ADOS. There are teams of specialists who diagnose autism, which might include some or all of the following: a developmental pediatrician, psychiatrist, psychologist, occupational therapist, speech pathologist, and possibly others. Such teams will be more common in larger cities and university settings. To find a psychologist who diagnoses autism, you can start by asking your doctor for a referral. The next option is to contact your school district's psychologist or the special education department for names of psychologists or clinics who diagnose autism. An internet search is also a good way to find such psychologists or diagnostic teams.

DSM-5 and Autism

The most recent version (5) of the *Diagnostic and Statistical Manual of Mental Disorders* was published in 2013 with a different way of looking at and diagnosing autism. The major changes to autism exclude Pervasive Development Disorder and Asperger's Disorder. Some people are not happy with this change and others are more accepting. As I understand it, the reason the changes were made was to create a more standardized method for assessing autism spectrum disorder. Previously, there were a number of techniques used by institutions and by professionals to make a diagnosis. Once the learning curve is well established with the new criteria, there should be more consensus and common ground among professionals as the new specifiers, as they are referred to, are applied to diagnostic measures.

Autism Spectrum Disorder Symptoms

As with all other sections of this book, when referring to symptoms from the Diagnostic and Statistical Manual of Mental Disorders the terminology is stated in less technical language. There are two specific areas of focus: social function and repetitive behaviors.

Social Communication and Interaction

Social and emotional perceptions and normal interactions with others are lacking. Understanding and sharing feelings as well as responding to others' feelings are either missing or minimal. Nonverbal communication such as eye contact, facial expressions and gestures are in short supply or they are not there at all. There is an inability to start, develop, and keep ongoing relationships with little if any shared play or possibly no interest in having friends.

Repetitive Behaviors and Interests

The child repeats movements, plays with objects, or repeats words or phrases. Examples would be repeating movements with fingers or other body parts, lining up toys in a certain order or saying the same words or sentences over and over. Such children might show intolerance to change of any kind whether it be routines or going places, etc. They tend to have an extreme reaction to what are called transitions or change from one activity to another, with regard to different food or time of day they eat, or all kinds of difficulty with something that is not done the same way each time. Interests are fixated on just a few things with extreme devotion to what is wanted and excessive reaction if unable to continue doing what is wanted. They tend to have a preoccupation with strange activities, doing them over and over for long periods of time. Some have a high sensitivity to or lack of reaction to environmental stimulus of the senses. Examples would be reaction to sounds or certain kinds of clothing textures or to foods. Some children exhibit excessive touching, smelling, or attraction to lights or objects. Others have a high tolerance to pain or hot and cold.

With each of these two categories above there is a rating scale to determine the severity of both. Within this rating scale there are three levels of severity. Level one identifies the least number of symptoms and requires the least amount of support from others. Level two requires more support for more symptoms, and level three requires the highest amount of support for these individuals. They are classified from mild, to marked, to severe in terms of the individual's challenges.

The final diagnostic measures consider several other factors from the level of verbal communication, for example normal speech to no speech at all. Diagnosticians consider possible genetic disorders, medical problems, environmental factors, and neurodevelopmental or mental disorders. Putting all these factors together and drafting an assessment will be the challenge of those who diagnose autism using the new criteria. It will be interesting, over time, to see how this comes together.

Resources

This is a brief overview of how autism is defined and diagnosed currently. I hope it has been educational. If you are in need of further information, there are so many websites and new information coming out on this subject. I hesitate to provide specific web addresses and books because over time new publications and changes in websites supersede older information. Talk to teachers, your doctor, and those who diagnose autism to inquire about books and websites. Do your own research online, and you may find exactly what you are looking for.

Temple Grandin is a well-known author and speaker at autism conferences. She has autism spectrum disorder and is a doctor of animal science at Colorado State University. She has several books worth reading if you want to learn more about autism spectrum disorder from someone who has the diagnosis. Autism Speaks is a national organization with a website at autismspeaks.org. Again, websites change, so it is always good to research online for the most up-to-date resources and information.

One of the pediatric developmental specialists I work with at traveling clinics has a son with autism, and he has recently written a book with other doctors on autism. It is called, *Autism Spectrum Disorders: What Every Parent Needs to Know*, published by the American Academy of Pediatrics.

Children and adults with autism spectrum disorder qualify medically for Supplemental Security Income or SSI through Social Security. One must also qualify financially, so I would advise someone considering applying for SSI to read the chapter entitled, SOME SUGGESTIONS IF YOU HAVE A CHILD WITH A SPECIAL NEED. On average, it takes six months for a determination of eligibility; however, the payments when someone qualifies are retroactive back to the day of application.

chapter four
PARENTING AND CONCERNS WITH CHILDREN

Being a parent is not easy, especially if you are a single-parent or have a child or children who are difficult to manage. With some children we recognize at a very early age that they will be a challenge as they grow older. We can see this as parents, as early as three or four months of age. I read the results of a study that was done many years ago where the parents of young infants were asked to rate their child for each of nine personality traits on a spectrum from one extreme to the other. An example would be to describe their child from non-irritable to very irritable. They discovered that parents could rate their child on each of these scales as early as five months of age. I believe most parents notice the specific types of personalities their children have early on and each child has distinct differences from his or her siblings. These differences are formed when they are very young.

If you have concerns about any of your children, it would be wise to consult a therapist for help. There are therapies designed for children from toddlers on up. I don't believe there is any age, no matter how young the child is, that asking questions of a professional therapist is too early.

I believe a good rule of thumb is if your child begins to have problems, keep your eye on the situation because basic problems are always normal. Do your best to show love and concern and, if his or her behavior continues to deteriorate from what I would call one stage to an even deeper stage of problematic behavior, then seek professional help. If your child is under six years of age I would highly recommend you seek out a child therapist who is proficient at play therapy. Some children older than six can also benefit from play therapy.

What is Play Therapy?

A play therapist is someone who works with young children with a lot of props. They generally have a good-sized tray of sand with play figures and toys which are used as tools to tease out what the child is experiencing. They also have dolls that are used to represent members of families, friends, or anyone in a child's life. They also have a variety of other toys and objects to help children play out different scenarios in their lives. This can be a very powerful and revealing way of looking into a child's world without the child knowing the therapist is doing so. When children start playing and acting out their lives, they start to demonstrate how they interpret their world. The therapist can then begin to understand what the problems are and then devise a plan to treat the child. They often will help the child by using the toys, figures, etc. to model appropriate behaviors that assist the child to see better ways to deal with stressful situations in life. This method can be very successful.

There was a made for television movie several years ago depicting a true story of a child who was on a visitation with his father. He put the child to bed in a motel room and set it on fire in an effort to kill his son as a method of revenge toward his former wife. The boy survived the fire but was severely burned. One scene in the movie showed a play therapist talking with the young boy in his hospital bed. The child had dolls in his hands, one representing his mother and the other his father. He began hitting the doll representing his father on the bed table over and over again. It was very dramatic as he kept hitting the table with greater force each time he hit it, expressing his anger toward his father. Over time, such a child can be helped to appropriately exhibit his or her anger and hopefully work through a process of healing emotionally and mentally.

Many children do not know or understand what they are feeling and act out in inappropriate ways in an attempt to express their anger or other feelings. Parents can be confused and uncertain what to do when such behavior comes from their child. When this is the case a competent play therapist can often times get to the bottom of such behaviors by using these techniques.

Play Therapy in Groups

I once saw a training video of a play therapy group of three and four year olds, being led by a therapist. He had puppets on both hands as he played out a scene where one puppet took a toy from the other puppet. The therapist was the voice for both puppets, one being rude and aggressive and the other passive. Then he asked for a volunteer to act out the same scene. Two of these little kids were able to repeat the same behavior very well. He then asked the group how it made them feel when someone does that to them. They all chimed in and said how bad it made them feel. They were all very much into the whole experience. He put the puppets on again and showed them how to behave appropriately. The first puppet asked the second if he could play with the toy. The other puppet said he could have it when he was finished playing with it and when he was done after a few seconds he gave the toy to the other puppet. Then he asked for volunteers to act out the better way to share toys. Most of the kids wanted to do this and they repeated the appropriate behavior with excellent results. The next question to the group was how they felt about the second example and they all liked it much better. Not only did they like it better but they had all been given the chance to model the better behavior. That was a powerful example of how this type of therapy can help children deal with unfair and unpleasant experiences in life.

Craig T. Mitchell, LCSW

Parenting Styles in Today's World

In today's world I have noticed that many young parents are concerned with parenting their children appropriately. In many ways the parents of today are more aware of being kind and loving to their children. I believe these people are trying to stay away from the more authoritarian and sometimes harsh approach to raising children they may have experienced in their childhoods. This is good and I hope it continues. There is one approach to parenting by some of these parents today that causes me great concern, which I see more and more as time progresses. I am referring to parents who allow their children to do whatever they please, no matter where they are. You have seen these families who have children running amuck in stores, social gatherings, church, school events, and in all public places. This is especially disturbing when people are gathered and someone is trying to speak and people are trying to listen. All the while children are running about, yelling and disrupting or a baby or toddler is crying and no attempt is made to take the child out or teach him or her how to act in public by being quiet, sitting still and not interrupting. Common courtesy seems to have been lost with these people. They obviously love their children, but for some reason they do not have the slightest understanding regarding how rude and disruptive their children are. It is like the parents have blinders on. For these parents, the children can do no wrong. Patience and tolerance has its place but not in these situations.

I see this in many aspects of life where behaviors swing from one end of the pendulum to the other; then, over time, it swings back again. There was a time when children were meant to be seen and not heard; punishment was swift and harsh and kids were not allowed to have an opinion. Thank goodness that has changed; however, with the changes in discipline in many families today it seems like there is a swing to the other side of the spectrum.

The end result of all this, "let them do what they want," is a developing trend of children having little respect for authority, rules, and proper behavior. When I get parents coming to me because they have concerns regarding their children's behavior, I have to take into consideration what they, as parents, are doing or not doing to encourage their children to misbehave. Do they think their child should not be disciplined because it would harm them? Are they so loving that they cannot discipline? Sometimes I see parents who were abused as children, and they will not discipline. I believe, along with the concept of personality disorders discussed in the chapter by the same name, there are parents who will not discipline because they don't believe their children can do any wrong. This is tragic because some of their children will grow up having no respect for other adults, including teachers and employers.

If you have a child with behavioral problems, the question to ask yourself as a parent is, "What is my philosophy about parenting and discipline?" Our children need our love and also appropriate discipline. Believe me; I have seen it all in the clinic where I practice from verbally harsh parents to totally oblivious parents who have children that need to be redirected by our staff because the parents won't prevent them from destroying property. They are not parents but more like casual observers, and they think their children's inappropriate behavior is funny and cute. This can lead to out of control behavior when the children become teenagers who have never had anyone say, "No," to them. When this happens it is very difficult to change the child's path. So how do you discipline, and do you discipline at all? This is especially important to ask yourself if you have a young child who is behaving badly. The next question would be what should you do as a parent? My answer to parents is very simple. LEARN HOW TO PARENT! How do you do this? I will tell you later on in this chapter after I have explained a few things.

Craig T. Mitchell, LCSW

If You Have a Child Who is Acting Out, Read This

Taking your child to a therapist is a good thing if his or her behavior is out of control or, as mentioned, if he or she is not self-regulating. However, is that where your responsibility ends? No not by a long shot! There are many parents who take their child to therapists and say, "Fix him or her up and send them back when you are done." The thing that every parent needs to know is that they, as parents, need to become the therapist for their child in the home. This is important; DO NOT forget this! If your child is declining to deeper levels of inappropriate behavior, referred to today as dysregulation, helping your children to self-regulate his or her emotions is something you, as a parent, need to learn how to do. If parents think an hour session each week with a counselor is going to be the answer, they are probably going to be disappointed. If we think children less than 12 years of age are going to get insights from therapy and be able to say to themselves when they start acting out, "Oh there I go acting out again. I need to think about this logically and use the skills my therapist taught me. My anxiety is increasing and I need to begin self-talk to stop myself from worrying, becoming angry, and inappropriate," Guess what? Not going to happen! Yes, therapy will help, but young children need 24-hour therapists, meaning someone who is with them the majority of each day. Any guesses who that would be? Yes! that means YOU the parent. Parents, you need to learn how to redirect your children's behavior because you are right there and can model correct behavior and encourage them at the exact moment when learning is so critical. This involves a lot of energy and teaching by repetition, but it is much more effective when you deal with each issue immediately when the teaching moment is in your control. You can make all the difference! I will explain how you can accomplish this shortly.

The same is true for teenagers; when they are out of control you can't force them to go to therapy and like it. Some will recognize they need help and may be willing to cooperate, but others will be anywhere from passive to outright defiant. I have been amused at the number of times I hear school personnel say that a child needs counseling. Have you ever seen what happens when a parent takes an unwilling child to a counselor and wants a cure? I have, and it does not work in the majority of these cases.

To recap, counseling is the catch all for teachers, school counselors, and principals everywhere for inappropriate behavior. For that matter, many of us say, "He or she needs counseling." Others say, "He or she needs discipline." It is usually said in more colorful language than mine here. Don't fall into the automatic belief that everything can be solved by counseling. It is recommended every day by many who have good intentions like taking an aspirin for a headache. We all know that aspirin is not the best drug for everyone with headaches. Just the same, counseling is not going to be the answer for everyone.

Why Doesn't Counseling Always Work?

Counseling, as I say throughout this book, is Insight Therapy where a person needs two elements in order to increase the odds of a favorable outcome. The first thing they need is to be mature and intelligent enough to get insights and the second is the motivation to want to change. Otherwise, we are wasting time and money. If a child does not want to cooperate, a counselor is no better at helping a child to change than is the parent. Sometimes a play therapist can make progress with a younger child because they use toys and other props to allow a child to better express what they are feeling in a playful environment. In these cases, the child simply begins to play with toys in front of a therapist, and over time the themes of their concerns begin to reveal themselves. A good play therapist can direct a child and help him or her to process and let go of issues and associated feelings. However, if a child decides not to cooperate, this won't work either.

Some children from approximately eight to older teenagers can also make progress when they don't want to cooperate if they have a counselor who sticks with it and establishes a good relationship with them. In these cases, the therapist can't usually go the direct route, asking questions and trying to teach the child. They need to engage the child through another approach by doing whatever the child likes to do, involving fun and friendly activities. I call this "Chocolate Shake Therapy," where the therapist takes the child to get a treat, and they just hang out and talk about anything that comes up. This can take weeks to months and can be expensive for the family. Remember, it is always worth a try if you can get the child to go willingly.

For some children, they may need time before they are ready for counseling. For others they may not be ready because they are angry and until they are tired of bucking the system at home or school or both they may never be ready while they are living at home. Sometimes kids have to get to rock bottom before they finally say I need some help. This might happen because they have no privileges left or because they become isolated and depressed. If you think a child is becoming depressed or anxious, it is important to take him or her to your primary care doctor for a checkup. Treatment may require medication to get the child back to a better state of mind. If this happens then he or she may be willing to get more help.

What to Do If a Child Won't Go to Therapy

We need to decide what action to take if the child won't cooperate. This depends on his or her age and the severity of the problem. If a child is at the point where you are afraid he or she might hurt himself, herself, or others or you think he or she may damage property then you may have to take him or her to an inpatient program. Depending on where you live and the resources available, this might mean the psychiatric ward of a hospital. This can be done by making an appointment with your pediatrician or primary care physician. Another way to access this help is by going directly to the emergency room at the local hospital. This is what should be done if a crisis is brewing. Don't wait; go in; let the experts decide, especially if you are afraid for the child or family member. Your doctor is probably the best resource for all the options available in your community, so a call to him or her is always a good idea. Rural areas are sometimes difficult to find the necessary resources but ask, don't sit and wonder. A call to the nearest emergency room, psychiatric ward, or doctor is always advisable. You may only be able to talk to the doctor's nurse or someone who can give the doctor a message. Insist on a return call from someone! If you don't hear back, then call the nearest emergency room for direction.

Never take a threat from a family member lightly. If someone is saying he or she is going to hurt himself, herself, or someone else, make the call to 911. If you are dealing with something that is not urgent, and you don't know where to go or what to do, then it is time to look for resources. Here are some ideas about how to find resources.

How to Find Resources for Counseling

In most communities you should be able to find a local mental health center. Many of these agencies are established in each county in some states or there may be only one facility for several counties in rural areas. Sometimes these mental health centers are hooked into a network of treatment centers that can see anyone in the community, and they may have affordable fees, called sliding fee scales which takes into consideration your income, family size, and even medical expenses, in some cases. In some places these mental health centers are only able to see patients who have Medicaid because they are mostly funded by Medicaid programs. This is unfortunate, and you may have to look more extensively to find an affordable counseling program. Many communities have such counseling centers that will be able to serve anyone who enters their doors; hopefully these programs have sliding fee scales.

EAP or Employee Assistant Programs

Some employers have what are called Employee Assistant Programs which give family members from three to eight sessions of therapy free of charge. Check and see if this is available through your employment. See the chapter in Book 1 entitled, HOW TO FIND A THERAPIST OR COUNSELOR, describing these programs in more detail.

If You Have Health Insurance

Health insurances may have what are called mental health benefits which will enable those who are covered to go to counseling. Usually, you will have a co-pay and you may only be able to go to counselors who are on their list of providers. Call your insurance company and ask them about these benefits and what your co-pay would be. You may have a mental health benefits phone number on the back side of your insurance card that you can call about what they provide.

Parents Need to Learn How to Become Their Child's Therapist

When I receive calls from people who are seeking therapy for their child, I review much of what I have just said above and then I tell them that they need to become the therapist for their child. As I have said, who is with the child most of the day? You, as the parents, are. This is especially true if you have young children. You need to deal with the consequences quickly when inappropriate behavior is displayed right in front of you. You are in the very best place to create consequences that are closely associated with the child's behavior so he or she will learn from his or her behavior that poor choices result in less than happy consequences. The opposite is also true; good choices result in much better consequences or outcomes. If we are consistent in providing reinforcement for good behavior and less than favorable consequences for inappropriate behaviors, then the child will, over time, begin to make the connection and start to change his or her behavior. This may not always be the result when mental illness or abuse is part of the picture, but in the majority of cases, it begins to work over time. This is a process because it takes time for a child to develop difficult behaviors, so it follows that it takes time and your strong will to see these changes through. Behavioral therapists have learned these skills and use them to produce better behavior in children. You can do the same!

Where Do You Learn to Be Your Child's Behavioral Therapist?

Where do you learn these skills? Do you go to college and get a degree in Child Psychology?

NO, YOU TAKE A PARENTING COURSE!! Don't moan or go cold on this advice because it can really give you confidence with skills that work with most children.

I taught a parenting course for over 10 years. I certified parents who had taken the course to actually teach it in their own communities. I have seen how sound parenting principles give parents hope and confidence and, when these methods are combined with consistency, they can produce amazing changes in their children and in themselves as parents.

WHY PARENTING COURSES CAN MAKE YOUR LIFE EASIER

Before Addressing this Statement We Have to Push Past a Major Roadblock for Parents to Even Consider a Parenting Course

First, let me say that there are a lot of parents out there, **especially fathers**, who think they know everything about parenting and there is nothing they can or should learn from anyone on the subject. They think this despite the fact that their child/children and spouse might be on the verge of disaster. They frequently don't think they had anything to do with the problem because they know best and the problem is with the child and not them, because they don't have problems with parenting. Again, this is most often the case with fathers, although there are mothers who think this way as well. I am very sure I had at least one father in every parenting class I taught that was dragged there by his wife. Have you ever stood up in front of a group of people, some of whom looked at you as if you were the enemy? That is literally what it was like, and I'm sure it is much the same today in similar parenting groups. However, I knew if I could keep them coming until the lesson on Natural and Logical Consequences, I had them! That was because by then it all came together and made sense to them. It gave them a whole different perspective on how to discipline with effectiveness that was very sound logically. We all became a team with the same goal in mind, to utilize proven techniques to enhance their capacity to change their child's behavior. In my experience, if we can get fathers to agree to attend a course they will be glad they did, especially if they keep an open mind and a desire to learn some new ideas.

Mothers and Wives, What to Say to Get Your Husband to Help Him Consider Going to a Parenting Class

I will say this in a number of areas throughout this book in order to get men to step up and do what is best for their families. Wives, tell your husbands that going to a parenting course is like going to Home Depot to learn how to lay tile or put up a fence. Whenever we want to learn how to do something around our homes, we go to the experts and take a class or seminar on the subject. We then purchase the materials and tools and go home and replicate what we have learned from the professionals to make the desired home improvements. That is exactly what we do when we want to make family improvements! We learn from the experts and then go home and use the tools and skills we have learned to change behaviors, in us and our children.

Consistency is Key in Parenting

When I talk to parents about parenting, I often emphasize a few principles that can make their experience with their children much more effectual. I come across a lot of parents who say they have read books or gone to parenting courses, but they tried it and it doesn't really work. When I hear this I believe the reason the concepts don't work is because the parents don't understand one major principle that is critical in parenting with any methodology. Without this principle no parenting theory will be effective. That principle is Consistency or "Stick-to-itiveness," if such a word exists. If you can say I am bigger, smarter, older, stronger, and more dedicated than my child and I will not give in, you come from a position of strength. Who is the parent? You are, and therefore you need to stay the course because if you do you will eventually see success. I then ask them if they ever let their children start their car or grab the steering wheel or light matches and they say no. I ask them why don't they let them and they say something like I won't allow it because it is too dangerous. **Oh, so you are saying when it comes to important and life threatening things you are consistent but with other things which aren't dangerous you allow them to happen? Over time, by not consistently dealing with problematic behavior it will drive us crazy as parents.** Do you get it? Most people who hear this in person get it. So one very important concept I want to emphasize is this: **We teach our children to do things that drive us crazy by our in inconsistency.**

When we tell a child he or she cannot have a cookie until after the next meal, what does the cookie beggar do? He or she throws a tantrum. These children know they can get a cookie when mom has company, when she is on the phone, or when in a store. All they have to do is throw a fit and all of the good intentions go out the window. Despite all the talk about no cookie till after dinner, if mom is on the phone she says to her child, okay here is the cookie; just go outside so I can talk on the phone. The happy child goes outside with the cookie and tells a friend all I have to do to get a cookie before dinner is cry or have a fit and she gives me one every time. The other child says, my mom won't ever do that and if I cry or have a fit she puts me in time out.

There are some exceptions to basic parenting principles, for example children who have special needs, but even with these special situations you can learn strategies that will work for you if you apply basic concepts learned in parenting courses or books. I will talk about these special circumstances in other chapters and where you might find additional direction. Right now, I will deal with only the average and highly difficult world of most kids. This covers a lot of territory because most of us are dealing with many difficult little personalities and situations with our children and that is normal! Still, with special needs children we also need consistency and much more of it!

Back to the people who say parenting books or courses don't work. I usually ask them a few questions about what did not work, and I believe most parents give up early because they don't get the desired results right away. Some might work at it a bit longer but aren't really invested or sold on the principles they learn. When they try them on their children they give up because children don't want to see things change so they resist any changes as hard as they can by increasing their unacceptable behavior. They do this because they want to stay in charge. That is when parents give up, believing the methods they have learned don't work.

This is why each parent must understand when starting new methods of dealing with misbehavior they will see their children react with escalating misbehavior. This is a fact every parent needs to accept. In order to make real change we have to PAY THE PRICE and say, "I will stick with this until I see results." At this point I tell parents about a couple who were neighbors to a psychology professor I had in college. I was taking a class on the Psychology of Learning, and the professor told us about a couple next door that had a young baby. They tried for many nights to put her to bed but she would always cry and tantrum until they picked her up and rocked her to sleep. She had trained her parents well, don't you think? They asked the professor what to do, and he asked them a few questions. Was the baby sick, was she fed properly, did she have a clean diaper? To all these questions they answered, yes. He then asked what happened when they picked her up from her crib, and they said she immediately stopped crying. He told them the reason she stopped crying is because she wanted to stay up and be rocked to sleep. He suggested that they put her down after making sure she was fed, not sick, and had a clean diaper and then they should ignore her until she went to sleep. He assured them that crying would not be harmful and that ignoring her did not mean they were bad parents; they were simply getting her used to a routine. He told them it would take about three nights to extinguish this behavior and although they had difficulty walking out the first night they decided to go ahead and try it.

The first night she cried for about 20 minutes. The next night she cried for about 30 minutes. The third night she cried for almost 15 minutes and the next night she fussed briefly and went to sleep. Her parents had effectively extinguished her behavior by being consistent and sticking with the program.

My Own Experiment with My Son

When I heard this in class I knew I needed to do the same with my oldest son. At that time he wasn't quite two years old. We had just put him in a single bed from a crib. Night after night when I put him to bed and closed the door he would get out of bed, run to the door laughing and knock on it. We tried everything we could think of to stop this behavior but nothing worked. The day my professor described the example above I reasoned that if I was going to teach the same methods for dealing with problematic behavior in my career, I needed to try it on my son. I realized that I would have to pay the price and be consistent until I got results. I was not going to give up. I was determined!

That night when I put him to bed I closed the door and stood there listening. I heard him getting out of bed and if I opened the door before his feet hit the floor, I would tell him to stay in bed and he would. If his feet touched the floor he would come running to me giggling with a big smile on his face. I did this for about 20 minutes the first night and he finally went to sleep. The second night I did the same thing for over 30 minutes and the third night just over 15 minutes and he did not get out of bed again. The battle was over, and it took me just over an hour of time over three nights to accomplish the task. It was a little inconvenient when I was involved in this process but, in the end, it was successful.

It wasn't till many years later that I realized why he was so happy and came running for me each night. When I used to come home in the evening he would come running and I would throw him in the air and we would hug and have a happy, fun reunion. He wanted to repeat this whenever he could. I realized it was a very positive reason he would not stay in bed, not because he was trying to be difficult. I am glad I made that connection. If we could all think about our children's behaviors in this manner to try and understand what motivates them to do what they do, we might be surprised with the insights we get.

The main point here is to emphasize that using sound principles of parenting with consistency and determination, you can make positive changes in your parent/child relationships.

More Examples of Consistency

As further evidence, I offer other examples to demonstrate how consistency works for parents. I can't tell you the number of times when my children were young that my wife and I had to tag team with each other to deal with our children's misbehavior. When we had a child that we knew was becoming a problem when going shopping, we would decide ahead of time, which of us would be the one to take the child back to the car in the parking lot if he or she misbehaved in a store. It was usually my boys who were the most challenging when they were young, so my memories are full of dragging them, sometimes literally, out to our vehicle. Following through when you set the rules is vital so we told them before leaving the vehicle they would get one warning inside the store; if behavior problems arose and they were warned and then it occurred again we would take them back to the car. No second or third warnings were allowed, and my wife and I backed up each other on this. We would occasionally tell them we would get a treat if their behavior was acceptable. I remember waiting a long time in the car on some of these occasions but my children learned that we meant what we said. We only had to do this once or twice for each child, and they got the message loudly and clearly.

A Point to Remember

Never make promises or tell the child you will do something if you do not have a plan to follow through. Giving warnings without a resolve to follow through teaches the child that you can be manipulated and that you don't mean what you say. In reality, they take over and keep pushing because they know you won't do what you say.

Another Point to Remember

If you want to change a child's behavior, you need to plan ahead of time when you know what the child is going to do in a certain situation (i.e. that your child will take off in a store). Be proactive and don't give up. Plan what you will do if he or she runs away and be willing to pay the price to change his or her behavior (i.e. having someone go to the car with the child as in my example). You may even want to plan a trip to a store just to put into motion this strategy. It will be well worth the time you take to ensure the child or children get your message. Be strong and don't be manipulated.

Single Parents

If you are a single parent it might mean you will go home a few times from a store and leave a shopping cart full of items. You can try going to the car and waiting until the child knows you mean business, then go in the store and try it again. Go right back out if the behavior happens again and just go home. If you are a single parent, arrange to have a plan B in place so if the child acts out you have someone to watch the child while you go back to the store and do your shopping. The child will then know if he or she does not act properly he or she won't go with you again. You will feel stronger, more confident, and your child's behavior will begin to change.

Parenting Classes are Actually Fun

When you take a parenting class you will have the opportunity to discuss examples of situations regarding your children with the instructor. Together you, others in the class, and the instructor will have fun discussing different ways of dealing with these behaviors. It can get very creative during these classes, and you will make good friends with the parents who attend with you.

The Drive to the Movie Theater: Another Example

A couple is driving their family to the movie theater and two of the kids in the back seat start to quarrel. After a minute of this the father asks them to stop the arguing. It continues so he warns them if they don't stop he will turn around and go home. The kids ignore this warning because dad has never followed through on this before and besides he really wants to see the movie. Therefore, they continue to hassle each other, and dad, along with mom, continue to throw out warnings and empty threats. Finally, they reach the theater and everyone is in a bad mood because they have all been engaged in an argument. The kids have no consequences for their behavior.

Rewind this scenario and picture the husband and wife discussing what they will do if the kids start to quarrel. They agree that if this happens they will return home and send the kids to their rooms and they might even have a babysitter lined up so they can return to the movie. When they are driving to the movie and the situation happens like the one above and after giving one or two warnings, they turn around and go back without any emotion, arguing, or hesitation. You have to be willing to sacrifice going to the movie for the sake of being consistent and in charge. It can be even more effective if the kids are old enough to stay home; then the parents can drop them off and head back to the movie. What do you think the kids will do next time?

Knott's Berry Farm

My favorite part of the parenting course I taught explained how we, as parents, are inconsistent causing ourselves more stress. Parenting is like playing slot machines. Do you know why people put quarters in slot machines over and over? It is because of inconsistency. I will explain by the following example included in that parenting course.

The story is told of a pig at Knott's Berry Farm who was trained to go down a slide, very often, all day long. I am adding to the story because I don't know all the exact methods used to train the pig, but I think I am probably close. The method of teaching the pig how to do this will explain the question, "Why do we, as parents, teach our children to do things that drive us crazy?"

The pig had to be trained by appealing to its appetite. I believe they probably consulted with a psychologist to do this training. The first step was to teach the pig that every time he heard a bell ring, food would be released into his feeding trough. After a while the pig learned that for some reason when the bell rang, food appeared. After a while, he would only be fed if he was looking in the direction of the stairway made of logs to the top of a slide. Gradually, his behavior was shaped so he would only be fed if he went to the top of the slide. I am sure the next step was to push him down the slide because most pigs would not go down a slide even if coaxed by food, at least the first time. When he slid down a trip bar attached to the slide was engaged causing the bell to ring and food was deposited in his tray. After getting him to go down the slide a number of times, the pig realized that for some reason when he hit the trip bar the bell would go off and voila, food would appear.

This was good because now he was trained to go down the slide. However, after going down the slide for several minutes he was no longer hungry, and he stopped going down the slide. People would walk by and wonder what the slide was doing in a pig pen. The idea was to have the pig going down the slide most of the day so they decided to give him food after going down the slide twice. The next time the pig went down I'm sure he panicked and went down again and to his delight he got his food. After a while he understood that he needed to go down twice for his food and it was not long before he was full and he stopped again. The trainers would have moved his schedule to three times and then maybe to every five times but despite this he would only go down the number of times it would take to get full and then he would stop. So how do you get an animal or human to do something all the time? Simple, you use the same method as casinos use to get people to throw away their money. They only give the reward on a variable schedule or in other words, who knows when, sometimes sooner, sometimes later. That is why the little old ladies, who should know better, keep putting their money in the slot machines because they know if they keep dropping coins in they will get their reward eventually. So when the pig's reward schedule was changed to, "whenever," he kept going down the slide over and over again, all the while thinking, "If I keep going down this slide I will get food eventually." This is how we reinforce any behavior, by rewarding it on a variable schedule: in other words, **inconsistency**. Parents do the same with children; by being inconsistent we teach our children to constantly badger us. If we say one thing and eventually, after being worn down we give in, we have given children the message that they should hound us until they get what they want.

The Cookie Beggar

For example, what if we tell a child, "You cannot have a cookie until after lunch," and the child throws a fit, becomes angry, and continues to beg for 10 minutes, causing us to become weak, give in and give him or her a cookie? Guess what we have done? We have taught the child to throw a fit and beg for cookies. Next time they will go 15 minutes or even longer because we have taught them that it takes at least 10 minutes or longer of begging to receive their reward. This is why the cookie beggar keeps driving mom crazy, even when she tells him or her, "No cookies until after dinner." Do you see now what mom has unknowingly done? She has taught him to beg for cookies over and over again until she is half crazy and then gives in. So what do we do to stop this process? When we make a rule, we stick with it and don't give in, like the child who lives next door to the cookie beggar. He asks the cookie beggar, "How did you get a cookie?" and he is told, "All I have to do is bug my mom until she gives me one." The other child says, "If I do that I never get a cookie and I get a time out if I keep asking."

This is a true principle of learning. When we do not reward inappropriate behavior and say to ourselves, I am stronger, smarter, older, and wiser and I won't give in, then the child will finally give up, and we have a won a great victory. It is like pushing a car up over a hill. It is hard to keep pushing because it is exhausting, but if we keep on track and stay committed on being strong, eventually our consistency will pay off; when we get to the crest of the hill the car will coast down the other side. Then we will have won an important battle with our children, and they will know that when we make a rule we will follow through. This is especially true if we have a child with a difficult temperament.

To emphasize the importance of parental consistency and how it interacts with a child's temperament, I include in this chapter a statement from Gerald R. Patterson Ph.D. I found this quote some years ago but I have been unable to identify where it is found in Dr. Patterson's works.

"Parenting style interacts with the child's temperament, either mediating or exaggerating the vulnerabilities. For example, parents who are impatient, inconsistent, and who use punitive and critical methods of parenting are most harmful to children with difficult temperaments.

Severe conduct disorders are difficult to treat. Although long-term follow-up studies have not proven their efficacy, behavioral and structured treatments, such as positive reinforcement, restriction of privileges, timeout, and overcorrection, appear to offer the most promise. Insight-oriented therapies have largely failed.

Therapies which can change parenting and family systems also offer promise. Targets for change include inconsistent and arbitrary parenting, explosive expressions of anger by parents, tense and frustrated mothers, emotionally distant fathers, extremes of restrictiveness and permissiveness, hostility and rejection by parents, severe physical punishment, and neglect. It may be critical to recognize aggressive chains precipitated step-by-step through inappropriate parental responses."

Four Reasons for Misbehavior

This is a concept taught in a parenting handbook and class called *STEP* or *Systematic Training for Effective Parenting*.[2] I like these ideas because they are true in my experience. These apply to younger children but also can be applied to older children to some degree.

---

2   Dinkmeyer, D. C. Sr., McKay, G. D., & Dinkmeyer, D. C. Jr. (2007). *The parents' handbook*. Fredericksberg, VA: STEP Publishers.

THE GOALS OF MISBEHAVIOR

Child's Faulty Belief	Child's Goal	Parent's Feeling and Reaction
I belong only when I am being noticed or served.	**Attention**	FEELING: Annoyed REACTION: Tendency to remind and coax
I belong only when I am in control or I am boss, or when I am proving no one can boss me!	**Power**	FEELING: Angry! Provoked! As if authority is threatened REACTION: Tendency to fight or to give in
I belong only when hurting others as I feel hurt. I cannot be loved.	**Revenge**	FEELING: Deeply hurt REACTION: Tendency to retaliate and get even
I belong only by convincing others not to expect anything from me. I am unable. I am helpless.	**Display of Inadequacy**	FEELING: Dispair, hopelessness, I give up REACTION: Tendency to agree with child that nothing can be done

This is powerful information in the hands of parents as they try to understand and deal with their children's behavior. If parents could just write these goals of misbehavior down and be consistent about responding to them, they would feel much more in control and have more confidence in redirecting their child's behavior. Currently, the description of teaching children how to control their emotions and behavior is called Self-Regulation. Just following this simple format will help parents become much more secure in dealing with misbehavior.

Child's Response to Parent's Attempts at Correction	Alternatives for Parents
Temporarily stops misbehavior. Later resumes same behaviors or disturbs in another way.	Ignore misbehavior when possible. Give attention for positive behavior when child is not making a bid for it. Avoid undue service. Realize that reminding, punishing, rewarding, coaxing and service are undue attention.
Active or passive-aggressive misbehavior is intensified, or child submits with defiant compliance.	Withdraw from conflict. Help child see how to use power constructively by appealing for child's help and enlisting cooperation. Realize that fighting or givin in only increases child's desire for power.
Seeks further revenge by intensifying or choosing another weapon.	Avoid feeling hurt. Avoid punishment and retaliation. Build trusting relationship; Convince child that she or he is loved.
Passively responds or fails to respond to whatever is done. Shows no improvement.	Stop all criticism. Encourage any positive attempt, no matter how small, focus on assets. Above all, don't be hooked into pity and don't give up.

Recap

One of the major messages of this chapter is to be consistent. Do not tell a child something if you do not intend to be true to your word. The other message is every parent should take a parenting course. If you do you will learn about these concepts and many, many others. You will learn parenting skills that have proven to be effective when dealing with children. You will be in a class setting that allows interaction between the instructor and all the others who are taking the course. You will also make friends with other parents who are trying to increase their understanding of children and to enhance their parenting skills. You will exchange ideas with these other parents that might just make a difference for you and your children. If you keep your mind open, you will be very glad you did. It is just like going to Home Depot and learning how to install a sink.

Another reason why couples will benefit from parenting courses is because when they complete a course they will both be on the same page and have a united front in the battle to out think and maneuver around the little rascals who live in their homes. This is true if you are willing to try the methods you learn for at least a year. If we are not united as one, we can, at times, be divided by our children.

Learning new parenting skills can be very simple if you will give the course a chance by going in with an open mind and listening objectively. If you do I can almost guarantee that you will find some gems in terms of strategies, as well as simple outlines to guide you in most situations you will experience with your children. You will also learn methods of parenting that take the guess work out of many situations because you will know how to approach everyday situations and also difficult scenarios with a greater sense of power and confidence as you interact with your children. I truly believe you will be happy you did. It is a given that each course has its own principles, but the concepts taught are somewhat similar in many of the courses offered. The important thing is that you go and have fun learning.

chapter five
DELAYED DEVELOPMENT IN CHILDREN

As much as 75% of the delays children exhibit cannot be explained nor a cause detected by today's technology. I have heard a pediatric neurologist tell parent after parent this statement as they were trying to find a diagnoses and answers as to why their children were falling behind peers or having problems in various areas of development.

Delayed Development

This includes the minor delays seen in many typically developing children such as speech and language delays. Some of these problems with receptive speech (understanding speech) or expressive speech (talking) can be caused by hearing loss and difficulties associated with ear infections or conditions at birth. Fine motor skill delays such as difficulty grasping and manipulating small objects and trouble with hand-to-eye coordination or eating are sometimes observed. These are the small muscle groups required for finer, more precise movements used in coloring, drawing, and writing, etc. Some delays involve gross motor skills such as rolling over, crawling, standing, walking, or any type of movement requiring the large muscle groups of the body.

Craig T. Mitchell, LCSW

Sensitivities Involving the Senses Causing Delayed Development

We also need to consider a different realm of atypical development with children who have high sensitivity to the senses like touch, involving reactions to the feel of clothes and textures. A child can be so irritated by the feel of a certain type of material that he or she will undress or take certain items of clothing off that are the source of their irritation. To a person without these feelings it would be like putting on socks or a shirt made of poison ivy or some other highly itchy or painful substance. Little wonder some of these children are so agitated and can throw tantrums for hours with no way of communicating what they are experiencing because they are too young to have developed speech, or they may be delayed in many areas including speech. They can also react to the taste or texture of certain foods, being unable to eat certain foods or many foods in general. More children than you would think have horrible reactions when presented with foods they find to be uncomfortable. They can react so strongly that they will tantrum just at the sight of the food item. Parents will sometimes mistakenly interpret this behavior with their child just being picky or spoiled. They may not understand that the child has real issues with how their brain processes the information received by their senses.

Some children can be sound sensitive and become agitated to noise such as sirens, vacuums, blenders or toilets. When any of these sounds occur the child might become inconsolable and may run and hide, have a tantrum, or act out in various ways. The child might scratch or hit himself or herself or possibly cry and rage for long periods of time, and the parents feel helpless because no matter what they do to intervene, nothing can calm the child down. These children are very interesting because they seem a little quirky and sometimes they are extremely difficult and frustrating because they don't respond to normal methods of calming. Many parents try using discipline which is ineffective because it does not address the real problem and may exacerbate the problem. Children with such sensitivities can even be very baffling to your doctor and other professionals who might have the opportunity to examine them. With the right diagnosis and the correct type of therapy, affected children can learn how to adjust and better cope with their problem. The professionals who are trained in diagnosing and treating these kinds of problems are Occupational Therapists. Some of these kids may be experiencing symptoms of autism and may need more extensive evaluations and help for a long period of time. If this is the case then a psychologist who is trained in testing for Autism Spectrum Disorders generally diagnoses these conditions.

Delays and Disabilities from Identifiable Causes

Traumatic brain injury or trauma at birth or later are problems which have an identifiable cause. Premature birth, birth defects, or genetic syndromes cause delays and disabilities, some of which are passed down from generation to generation and others just happen. A "congenital anomaly," is another term used to describe any kind of birth defect, genetic or abnormal development in the womb. Some children contract diseases causing disabilities or delays while they are infants. Some disabilities are more subtle and don't show up until a child is older (from 2 to 5 years of age) such as mild cerebral palsy or symptoms from premature birth. Mothers are very insightful when it comes to being aware of these concerns. They often have feelings, impressions, and worries about a child before others ever suspect anything is not right. If there are mothers out there who have such feelings, I would encourage them to have their child evaluated by appropriate professionals starting with their pediatrician or family doctor. The earlier the better unless the child is too young for a complete evaluation, including cognitive (brain) function because diagnosing an infant can be tricky.

Motivated Moms Are Amazing Advocates for Their Children. Don't Get in Their Way!

I met a mother at a traveling clinic, and she was the only one who felt something was wrong with her son. She finally pushed to have him seen by one of our psychologists, and he was diagnosed with Asperger's Syndrome. Even though she was saddened by the diagnosis, this mother was so relieved that she had worked hard to get someone to listen until her concerns were confirmed. When I told her she is one of these mothers who choose to act on her impressions regardless of what others might think, she began to smile because she had run into resistance from her husband, and she felt vindicated. THANK GOODNESS FOR PERCEPTIVE MOTHERS!

Some of these children lag behind in various areas of development and then suddenly, and with no apparent reason, they start to develop as if a switch had been turned on. I see a lot of this in the clinic where I work. Some people expect children who are premature to develop at the same pace as a full-term child. I don't know how many times I have heard stories about grandparents, family members, or friends who compare a premature child to other children and imply that they are not being fed or taken care of adequately. This is the source of a considerable amount of guilt in mothers who may not understand that a premature child or one that has had birth trauma needs to be measured by different criteria. Premature growth charts have been created to properly follow the progress of normal development for a premature infant. We occasionally see doctors' offices using the same growth charts for children born full term, to plot height, weight and head circumference for premature children. This can create a lot of unnecessary stress and guilt especially when a trusted health care professional raises concerns because a premature child is compared to typically developing children. A smart parent who has a child born prematurely or one who has had some kind of birth trauma would do well to ask if their child's growth chart is for premature infants.

Second Opinions and Pediatric Developmental Specialists

I also hear of parents whose doctors tell them nothing is wrong with their child only to later find out that indeed there were conditions which should have been explored. If you, as a parent, have concerns about your child, and you believe your doctor is not addressing these concerns, it is perfectly appropriate for you to seek a second opinion from another doctor. In such cases, if it is feasible, you may want to search out a Pediatric Developmental Specialist. This is a doctor whose specialty is looking very closely at the child's overall development to determine if they are on track or if any red flags or concerns can be identified. I would encourage every parent to trust their instincts until they are satisfied that their concerns have been addressed.

chapter six
IDENTIFYING NORMAL AND DELAYED DEVELOPMENT IN CHILDREN

Do You Have a Child with a Problem?

If you are such a parent, you may know something is not right with your child but you don't know what to do about it. You might be thinking, "Where do I go to get help and how do we pay for it?"

I have seen a number of mothers who have children with developmental delays or other problems, only to be told that nothing is wrong when they receive an evaluation. This is especially true if the child is young because it is difficult to detect problems when children are very young due to not having developed enough to measure their progress. These mothers have a deep intuitive sense about them. They search for answers and only after time when the problems become apparent do others and possibly even doctors finally see what the mother has always believed. I realize there are some mothers who are overly concerned and they can be mistaken, but at the very least they should have their children assessed if only to rule out their worries. Then there is the case of a parent who wants to find something wrong with their child, which fortunately is rare. Thank goodness for loving mothers and fathers who do all within their power to see that their child receives all the help and treatment they need.

Some parents just do not know where to turn for answers, and they feel helpless and hopeless. To illustrate how this feels, if you are a parent, you may remember a medical emergency involving your child and you had no idea what to do. Let's consider a real life example such as the first time your child choked on something or had a bad cut or a broken bone. I recall my first brush with an emergency involving my oldest daughter. She was about three years old at the time. I was at home alone with my two children and noticed that she picked up a penny, and before I could get to her she swallowed it. She began choking and I had no clue what to do. I picked her up and ran across the street to our neighbor. Luckily, this experienced mother was there and she began slapping her on the back. This was horrifying! After a few moments she swallowed the penny. Knowing she swallowed it alarmed me; however, it was much better than watching her choke. At this point this kind and wise mother assured me that in a few days the penny would pass through her system and that she would be alright. She was correct. I can still remember how it felt to be so helpless. If you have been in a similar situation I'm sure you can conjure up that feeling by just thinking about it.

I relate this experience to help us all understand what it is like for parents with a child who has mental, emotional, medical, or learning problems or who has a disability. Parents often feel helpless as they struggle with what to do. I recall a very good mother who came to the clinic where I work many years ago. She brought her infant son to be evaluated. The eventual diagnosis was severe cerebral palsy, meaning that her son would be in a wheelchair and would never have the ability to walk or speak. After about two years of attending our clinic and seeing our doctors, she very humbly asked, "When will my son be cured?" It was heart wrenching to tell her that there was no cure for his medical condition. We all want to make sure our children are safe and have all their needs taken care of at the highest levels. We can start by making sure we are aware of anything that might indicate our child has a problem of any kind and then be proactive enough to start asking questions and looking for answers. We can do this by talking to our doctor, school, or other parents and searching on the internet.

Where Can We Start to Look for Answers If We Think Our Child Is Not Developing Normally? Let's Start with Milestones.

What are Milestones?

Milestones are certain skills a child would normally be expected to do at various ages. These can also be called stages of development. The following milestone information is taken from a brochure from the Utah Department of Health/Child Development Clinic. The following milestones are to help you decide where your child is based on these normal expectations.

If your child is behind in any of these milestones you should discuss your concerns with your primary care physician, family doctor, or pediatrician. Sometimes children can be delayed in one or more of these criteria and will catch up on their own. Other children may need help to improve these skills before they become school age. For some children delays may point to more significant problems requiring medical intervention and other therapies.

Age	Social and Emotional	Feeding and Nutrition
birth	Likes to get attention by crying. Quiets when picked up. Looks at faces and others. Begins to wiggle around.	Instinctive feeding and sucking. Breast milk (or formula) is total diet. Needs to feed every 1.5 to 2 hours. Stomach and intestines immature; can't handle other foods.
3 months	Plays and smiles with mother. Can sleep through the night. Grasps with hands. Responds to light and sounds. Can imitate faces.	Mature sucking pattern. May bite nipple with gums. Usually less fussy, intestines going through development. May be ready for spoon by 4-6 months.
6 months	Begins to tell between mother and strangers. Becomes upset when separated from mother. Tries to feed self. Puts objects in mouth a lot. Can sit without help.	Spoon feeds foods that have been put through a blender. Up and down jaw movement. Opens mouth to anticipate spoon. Puts toys in mouth.
9 months to 1 year	Plays peek-a-boo and back and forth games with mother. Looks for and moves familiar objects. Explores more. Pays more attention and interacts with family. Enjoys parents' voice or reading.	Uses cup 1-2 sips at at time. Finger feeds using thumb and forefinger. Eats more food and texture (chopped foods, mashed table foods). May prefer to feed self.

Age	Motor (Movement)	Understanding and Talking
birth	Lifts head and turns to both sides by laying on tummy. Can hold head up briefly. Stiffens legs to stand on feet. Grasps briefly. Brings hands to head and face.	Startles or cries at noises. Awakens at loud sounds. Makes cooing and throaty sounds "gu." Makes sucking sounds. Makes pleasure sounds which consist of soft vowels.
3 months	Pushes upon forearms on tummy. Rolls from back to side. Reaches and grasps toys, blanket. Sits with support.	Smiles when spoken to. Seems to know parent's voice. Cries differently for different needs. Repeats the same sounds a lot.
6 months	Stands with full weight on feet with hands held. Belly crawls. Sits alone using hands for support. Transfers toy hand to hand. Shakes and bangs toys. Grasps toes. Rolls.	Makes lots of different sounds. Responds to name. Notices and looks around when hearing new sounds. Turns head toward the side where the sound is coming from.
9 months to 1 year	Crawls. Clasps hands. Takes toys out of a box. Pulls to stand. Walks along furniture. Walks with hands held. Pokes finger into holes. Can grab and hold Cheerios. Begins to put toys in or on	Says 2-3 words at age 1. Uses jargon (babbling that sounds like real speech). Enjoys listening to people talking. Listens to simple commands. Stops an activity when "No no" is said. Waves goodbye.

Printed by permission of the Utah Department of Health

Age	Social and Emotional	Feeding and Nutrition
1 1/2 to 2 years	Says "no" and responds to "no." Plays along with small objects. Explores with greater distance from parents. Requires an adult to watch for safety.	May show independence through food. Eats most people foods. May go through picky stages. Uses cup; scoops with spoon; begins using fork. Drinks from cup/glass without help.
2 1/2 to 4 years	May not like being away from parents. Will play side-by-side with children that are the same age. Starting to work together during play. Success in toilet training. Uses objects for comfort (blanket, teddy bear, etc.) More dreams and nightmares.	Able to chew most raw foods; could choke Feeds self with fork and spoon. Growth slows; appetite may decrease. Drinks from a straw.
5 years	At ease away from home for part of day. Shows likes and dislikes for friends, TV, activities, etc. Works together with friends and groups. Can accept short time-outs. May still be afraid of some things, like the dark.	Eats a variety of foods. Needs 3 meals and 1-2 snacks every day. Acts appropriate at table; mealtime 15-20 minutes.

Age	Motor (Movement)	Understanding and Talking
1 1/2 to 2 years	Crawls or walks up and down stairs. Runs. Kicks and throws ball. Begins to climb. Stacks toys or cubes. Puts shapes in shape sorter. Scribbles.	Has 10-15 words at 18 months. Uses 1-2 work questions ("Where kitty? Go bye-bye? More?) Puts 2 words together ("more cookie")
2 1/2 to 4 years	Jumps. Stands on 1 foot. Hops. Catches a ball. Rides a tricycle. Uses scissors. Likes to use one hand more than the other. Laces. Copies shapes in drawing.	Says most sounds except perhaps r, s, th, I and blends. Can repeat sentences made up of 12 syllables. Uses 200-300 words. Uses 2-3 word sentences. Asks lots of "why" and "what" questions. Uses the sounds p, b, t, d, w, h, n, m, & ya correctly.
5 years	Stands on 1 foot for 10 seconds Jumps 10 inch hurdle. Bounces and catches a ball. Skips. Drop kicks a ball. Walks on balance beam. Wants to be like adults; helps with kitchen tasks. Copies four letter words. Builds a six block design. Buttons, zips, and ties.	Says all sounds correctly except perhaps r, s and th. Hears and understands most speech in the home. Can answer about past, present, and future events.

Printed by permission of the Utah Department of Health

If your child is behind in any of these milestones you should discuss your concerns with your primary care physician, family doctor, or pediatrician. Sometimes children can be delayed in one or more of these criteria and will catch up on their own. Other children may need help to improve these skills before they become school aged. For some children delays may point to more significant problems requiring medical intervention and other therapies.

Hearing Problems

Because of a nationwide effort the past several years, most babies have their hearing tested if they are born in a hospital, prior to being released. If a problem is identified it should be dealt with immediately. There are some infants who pass their hearing tests at birth but develop hearing loss later.

Causes of Hearing Loss

Measles, mumps, and meningitis can cause hearing loss in infants. If there is a family history of hearing loss in your family it is more likely to happen to your child than in the average population. Multiple ear infections are a common cause of hearing loss. The most common cause of hearing loss in infants is middle ear infection and fluid retention. If your child has three or more ear infections, or if his or her hearing comes and goes you should see your doctor or an audiologist (someone who tests hearing). If you believe your child is not hearing normally then it is critical that you have him or her tested and treated. If not, his or her speech and language development can be delayed during these important early years of the child's life.

The Next Step

If you go to your health care provider and he or she believes your child has delays which are more concerning, he or she may refer you to seek further evaluation and possibly treatments by other providers. The more common referrals you might receive include the following: audiologists, speech pathologists, occupational therapists, and physical therapists. Audiologists test hearing. Speech pathologists/therapists test speech and provide speech therapy. Occupational therapists evaluate sensitivities to

textures, foods, sounds, and they also work with the small muscle groups, referred to as fine motor skills in the hands and fingers. Physical therapists assess the large muscle groups of the body called gross motor skills. These are therapists who help children learn how to roll over, sit up, crawl, and walk. There are also specialists in developmental pediatrics who look very specifically at the milestones above and determine where a child is according to his or her age in several areas of development. Your doctor may want you to see one of these doctors if he or she is not sure what is going on and he or she wants a second opinion from an expert. You may also be referred to a medical doctor who specializes in genetics to determine if your child has a medical condition that can be identified. In any case, your doctor should be leading the way for you to get as many answers as possible.

The Early Intervention Program/Birth to Three Years

Whether or not your doctor refers your child to one of the specialists above, you may want to have your child screened by what is called the Early Intervention Program. This is a program that is nationwide, and it exists to identify children from birth to 3 years of age who have delays in their development. They evaluate a child in several areas of development, and if a child is delayed enough they will provide therapy to hopefully improve the child's skills. Usually, the therapies they provide are speech, physical, and occupational. In my area, the actual therapy is done in the home of the child being served. Some of these early intervention programs have nurses and social workers that follow children until they are three years of age to make sure they are not falling behind on their milestones. Depending on where you live, this program may be called by different names. In order to find this program, ask your doctor or call your local school district and ask them if they know where to find it. The Early Intervention Program is often part of or coordinated within local school districts. Also, the special education department of school districts may be able to provide you with contact information to this program. You may have to tell them that the program you are looking for serves children from birth to three years of age who have developmental delays. If the school district does not have knowledge of this program, then you should call your local health department. The labor and delivery department or neonatal intensive care unit of hospitals may also know who to contact because they refer patients to these programs.

The Preschool Program or Development Preschool: Three to Five

There is another program for children with delays from three to five years of age which is called the Preschool Program. It may be called something different where you live. If a child in the Early Intervention Program turns three and requires additional therapy for delays they are transitioned into the Preschool Program. In my state both of these programs are operated through the school districts so the process to get a child into the Preschool Program from Early Intervention is simple.

These Preschool Programs differ from district to district, but most provide three hours of preschool experience four days a week for these children. Depending on the child's delays they may receive speech, occupational, or physical therapy as well as a focus in a classroom setting to enhance their cognitive, speech, and self-help skills. In my area transportation is also provided for children who qualify for this program. If you have a child in this age range who appears to have delays, then you should contact your doctor or school district and inquire about this program. This is another federal program, and each state receives funds to administer its mandates to help children maximize their potential prior to kindergarten. Your doctor should be aware of these programs and should refer your child to them if it appears they are in need of help to catch up with their peers.

Costs of These Programs

In the state where I reside, until about five years ago the Early Intervention Program was free of charge. Now there is a minimal fee for these in-home therapies, based on family size and income. Those who have Medicaid are not charged. The Preschool Program here has no fee to the family. It will be different in each state.

Private Therapy for Developmental Delays

Some parents want their children to have more therapy than they receive from these two programs. There are private rehabilitation clinics which provide speech therapy, physical therapy, and occupational therapy for children with developmental delays. Some of these clinics provide therapy for all ages and types of needs and others are specific to only work with children or surgery patients. Insurance companies have contracts with such clinics and might pay for your child or a family member to receive these therapies. If you have health insurance and you want more therapy for your child, check with them to see if they will pay for these benefits. Your primary care physician will probably have to write a referral describing what is called "medical necessity" in order for the insurance company to pay. Medical necessity is the proof the doctor provides through his or her comments to satisfy to the insurance company that the therapy is medically necessary. This can be hard to prove depending on the regulations insurance companies have. Medicaid may or may not pay for therapy because they also have many rules regulating what therapies they pay for. If you have Medicaid, ask your caseworker about their requirements for the kind of therapy your child needs.

Medical Home for a Child with Special Needs

If you have a child with a special need, you should look for a doctor who has a practice called a Medical Home. This is also called Patient-Centered Medical Home or PCMH. Doctors and medical clinics that have been designated as a medical home have a desire to serve children and other family members with special needs. With most doctors or clinics, you have probably noticed that appointments are scheduled very close together so you don't have a lot of time with the doctor or provider. With a medical home appointment times are much longer so the provider can deal with the complex issues that a patient with special needs presents. The bottom line is that your provider will be meeting with you and your child or family member for longer and more in-depth exams. You will be able to ask more questions and as a team, plan the future of your loved one.

Usually, a medical home is supposed to provide a case manager to assist patients with any care the provider recommends, such as a referral to a specialist. When you have a question, you can call the office and speak to the case manager, and they can ask the doctor or provider if you need a quick answer. If you want to find a medical home, you should search online for one in your area.

The following is the Immunization Schedule for Children from Birth to 6 Years from the Center for Disease Control:

Identifying Normal & Delayed Development in Children

Vaccine-Preventable Diseases and the Vaccines that Prevent Them

Disease	Vaccine	Disease spread by	Disease symptoms	Disease complications
Chickenpox	Varicella vaccine protects against chickenpox.	Air, direct contact	Rash, tiredness, headache, fever	Infected blisters, bleeding disorders, encephalitis (brain swelling), pneumonia (infection in the lungs)
Diphtheria	DTaP* vaccine protects against diphtheria.	Air, direct contact	Sore throat, mild fever, weakness, swollen glands in neck	Swelling of the heart muscle, heart failure, coma, paralysis, death
Hib	Hib vaccine protects against Haemophilus influenzae type b.	Air, direct contact	May be no symptoms unless bacteria enter the blood	Meningitis (infection of the covering around the brain and spinal cord), intellectual disability, epiglottitis (life-threatening infection that can block the windpipe and lead to serious breathing problems), pneumonia (infection in the lungs), death
Hepatitis A	HepA vaccine protects against hepatitis A.	Direct contact, contaminated food or water	May be no symptoms, fever, stomach pain, loss of appetite, fatigue, vomiting, jaundice (yellowing of skin and eyes), dark urine	Liver failure, arthralgia (joint pain), kidney, pancreatic, and blood disorders
Hepatitis B	HepB vaccine protects against hepatitis B.	Contact with blood or body fluids	May be no symptoms, fever, headache, weakness, vomiting, jaundice (yellowing of skin and eyes), joint pain	Chronic liver infection, liver failure, liver cancer
Influenza (Flu)	Flu vaccine protects against influenza.	Air, direct contact	Fever, muscle pain, sore throat, cough, extreme fatigue	Pneumonia (infection in the lungs)
Measles	MMR** vaccine protects against measles.	Air, direct contact	Rash, fever, cough, runny nose, pinkeye	Encephalitis (brain swelling), pneumonia (infection in the lungs), death
Mumps	MMR** vaccine protects against mumps.	Air, direct contact	Swollen salivary glands (under the jaw), fever, headache, tiredness, muscle pain	Meningitis (infection of the covering around the brain and spinal cord), encephalitis (brain swelling), inflammation of testicles or ovaries, deafness
Pertussis	DTaP* vaccine protects against pertussis (whooping cough).	Air, direct contact	Severe cough, runny nose, apnea (a pause in breathing in infants)	Pneumonia (infection in the lungs), death
Polio	IPV vaccine protects against polio.	Air, direct contact, through the mouth	May be no symptoms, sore throat, fever, nausea, headache	Paralysis, death
Pneumococcal	PCV vaccine protects against pneumococcus.	Air, direct contact	May be no symptoms, pneumonia (infection in the lungs)	Bacteremia (blood infection), meningitis (infection of the covering around the brain and spinal cord), death
Rotavirus	RV vaccine protects against rotavirus.	Through the mouth	Diarrhea, fever, vomiting	Severe diarrhea, dehydration
Rubella	MMR** vaccine protects against rubella.	Air, direct contact	Children infected with rubella virus sometimes have a rash, fever, swollen lymph nodes	Very serious in pregnant women—can lead to miscarriage, stillbirth, premature delivery, birth defects
Tetanus	DTaP* vaccine protects against tetanus.	Exposure through cuts in skin	Stiffness in neck and abdominal muscles, difficulty swallowing, muscle spasms, fever	Broken bones, breathing difficulty, death

* DTaP combines protection against diphtheria, tetanus, and pertussis.
** MMR combines protection against measles, mumps, and rubella.

2016 Recommended Immunizations for Children from Birth Through 6 Years Old

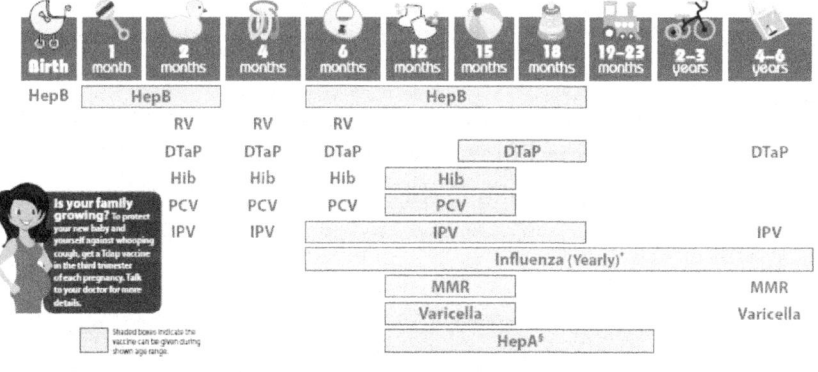

NOTE: If your child misses a shot, you don't need to start over, just go back to your child's doctor for the next shot. Talk with your child's doctor if you have questions about vaccines.

FOOTNOTES:
- Two doses given at least four weeks apart are recommended for children aged 6 months through 8 years of age who are getting an influenza (flu) vaccine for the first time and for some other children in this age group.
- Two doses of HepA vaccine are needed for lasting protection. The first dose of HepA vaccine should be given between 12 months and 23 months of age. The second dose should be given 6 to 18 months later. HepB vaccination may be given to any child 12 months and older to protect against HepA. Children and adolescents who did not receive the HepA vaccine and are at high-risk, should be vaccinated against HepA.

If your child has any medical conditions that put him at risk for infection or is traveling outside the United States, talk to your child's doctor about additional vaccines that he may need.

For more information, call toll free
1-800-CDC-INFO (1-800-232-4636)
or visit
http://www.cdc.gov/vaccines

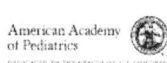

Craig T. Mitchell, LCSW

The Following are Trackers from The Center for Disease Control for Immunizations and Milestones:

[Immunizations and Developmental Milestones for Your Child from Birth Through 6 Years Old chart, showing recommended immunizations (Hepatitis B, Rotavirus, Diphtheria/Tetanus/Pertussis, Haemophilus influenzae type b, Pneumococcal, Inactivated Poliovirus, Influenza), milestones, and growth tracking from Birth through 6 Months.]

The information on these last two pages is taken from the U.S. Department of Health and Human Services, Center for Disease Control and Prevention website. I hope this information has been helpful to you and your family.

chapter seven
CHILDREN WITH SPECIAL HEALTH CARE NEEDS

What is a Special Need?

A special need can be as simple as any concern you have about your child. From one end of the spectrum this might be a delay in an infant who does not respond to your efforts to engage and talk to him or her, to speech, hearing, eating, rolling over, or any other milestone your child is not meeting. More serious problems might range from autism spectrum disorder to very severe disabilities and obvious medical problems and diagnoses.

State Programs for Children with Special Health Care Needs

In my state the department of health had an agency called Children with Special Health Care Needs (CSHCN). When I became employed with this department in 1991, I was shocked by what this agency had to offer. I had no idea that there was so much available for families who had children with special needs. At that time, we had specialists in pediatrics, neurology, orthopedics, genetics, cardiology, psychology, audiology, speech, occupational therapy, physical therapy and social work. It was my responsibility to refer families who came to our clinic to other resources and programs for their children. I had not been exposed to this arena of health care before, and I had to learn quickly what was available for children and families with disabilities. This was back before the internet, and it took a while to get a handle on what was out there for families in terms of resources. Some communities have good resources and others have very few. Keeping updated on all the programs available is the real trick.

Wherever you live you will probably have some kind of program to assist families who have special health care needs. In the United States there are federal funds which support these programs. In your area any programs available will probably be called by a different name. Often these programs are administered or overseen by the state or county and they either provide services or they contract with providers to do so. In other countries and in the United States, a web search with the words "children with special health care needs programs" should help identify where to go for services. There used to be so much more available, but funding for these programs is collapsing. The other advantage of a state-run agency is that a sliding fee scale is in place, reducing the costs to patients. In many of the cases seen at our clinic, families do not pay for their services beyond what their insurance covers.

As I understand it, each state has a similar program and legislatures choose how to administer these funds. The legislatures also decide if the state will contribute more funds to enhance the services available. Most states contract these services out to providers such as Health Management Organizations (HMOs). Other states choose to provide direct services to patients. This was the case in my state. Some states do not provide direct services and only refer people to other existing programs and resources. Rural areas may have few, if any, local resources for people with disabilities. Just getting an evaluation to determine a disability can be daunting when living in a small town.

A mother may believe something is not right with her child and she worries. Who is there to answer questions? The family doctor or pediatrician should know if there are specialists available and where to find them.

Children with Special Health Care Needs

Until just prior to publishing this book my state chose to provide direct services. Our staff traveled to several areas of the state to provide a number of specialty medical services to families. When I first started working with CSHCN, there were seven different areas in which we provided these services throughout the state. I was assigned to travel to four of these itinerant (traveling) clinics three times per year. The staff would be flown by plane to these sites for two days of clinics. We utilized the state aeronautics, which exists to provide transportation services to all state agencies. Flying staff is much more cost effective because we are within an hour flying time to most sites; therefore, we are not paying doctors and other staff for a day's travel to and from a site. Travel for the first clinic day begins by flying out by 7:00 AM in order to arrive at the clinic site and start seeing patients by 8:30 or 9:00 AM.

Our teams in the early 1990s included two pediatricians, two psychologists, a neurologist, a geneticist, an audiologist, a speech pathologist, an occupational therapist or physical therapist, two social workers, and one or two nurses. We also had an orthopedic surgeon who traveled to these areas two or three times per year, but they would travel on a different schedule than the team described above. We have another clinic called the Orofacial or Craniofacial team which consists of a plastic surgeon, an otolaryngologist (ear, nose, and throat surgeon), orthodontist, audiologist, speech pathologist, and social worker. This clinic is for children with cleft lip and palate or other disorders of the face and head. They traveled out to these itinerant clinics more frequently than they do today. We used to have Cardiology for children with heart defects but no longer. Now families have to travel to a special children's hospital for these services. CSHCN also has a clinic for Spina Bifida patients held at a children's specialty hospital three times per month.

These clinics have been a great blessing to the families in remote areas of the state including one area we visited on a Native American Reservation. These people have little exposure to specialty services, and if we did not provide them they would have to travel many hours to be seen. This usually translates into at least a two or three day journey for most families because of the distances involved. Staying overnight in a hotel can make it very stressful financially for many families. Sometimes in these cases we are able to arrange a stay at a Ronald McDonald House for a minimal fee.

How Things Have Changed

Several years ago our agency contracted with local health departments throughout the state to provide care coordination services at the local level. Potential patients called their local health department and spoke to a nurse about their concerns and appointments were scheduled with the team. This was a decided advantage and because of this arrangement we didn't send nurses to these traveling clinics. Beginning in 2010, because of budget cuts, two of these itinerant clinics were closed and attached to other clinics. The patients effected by these closures traveled an additional hour or longer to attend another clinic site. One of these clinics was reduced to a one day clinic three times per year. In the past we maintained three separate full time offices; however, with more budget cuts one of these offices was closed. Those patients had to travel about 40 to 50 miles or further to be seen at our main office. Until recently our itinerant clinics took one or sometimes two pediatricians, two psychologists, a neurologist, geneticist, audiologist, speech pathologist, occupational therapist, and social worker. An orthopedic doctor and physical therapist continued to visit some of these areas once or twice a year on a different schedule.

Our main office was located next to a major children's hospital, and we contracted with specialists at this hospital who are employed by a major university medical school to see our patients at our local and itinerant clinics. Over the years, as costs went up, we received less and less clinic hours from this contract because our budget remained the same or was even reduced. As our staff retired or left the agency, very few positions were replaced. This happened despite increases in many medical, developmental, and psychological problems in infants and children we see at increasing rates.

Recently the state closed our program and a state university hospital took over providing special needs services. How this program will look and provide for children with special needs and their families remains to be seen. What this means for the future of families with special health care needs is one of my greatest concerns. Unfortunately, it is a trend nationally for states to stop providing direct services to these needy families. I believe this kind of change will give less time for these complicated patients with their providers to come in line with corporate medical practice focused on getting patients in and out in very short, limited appointments. Unfortunately, much more time is required to adequately address special needs. We have all seen how this goes nowadays as we are rushed in and out of the doctor's office.

What is a Ronald McDonald House?

A Ronald McDonald house is a sort of basic hotel which can accommodate parents and a child who have to travel to obtain medical services, surgeries, etc. These facilities are usually located close to a specialty hospital, and the arrangements to stay are made by a hospital social worker. Usually, the cost to stay is much less than a hotel. There is usually a common kitchen so each family can prepare their own meals to reduce expenses. If you need to travel to such a hospital requiring an overnight stay, contact the social work department of the hospital to inquire if there is a Ronald McDonald House available, and they should be able to arrange for you to stay. Some hospitals have their own guest quarters for families of patients, so it would be wise to ask if there are such accommodations available.

Where to Look for a Special Needs Agency in Your Area

The best place to start looking for an agency to evaluate a child with special needs is usually with your doctor, pediatrician, or health clinic. If they do not know of such a resource, then contact your state, county, or provincial health department. Even if you live in a small town you may find that a team of specialists might visit somewhere close by on a regular basis. Hopefully, you won't have to travel to some distant city for an evaluation.

If you have a teenager or adult member of your family with special needs, you have noticed that I am focusing more on children in this part of the book in terms of medical diagnosis and treatment. The reason is that early diagnosis for children is critical in order to intervene and provide treatment to maximize the child's potential. When children enter their teenage years, usually they have been diagnosed and are in need of programs to teach them specific skills in order to become more self-sufficient. Many special needs teenagers require what are called Life Skills which teach them how to ride buses, count money, and purchase needed items. These skills are called Activities of Daily Living or ADLs.

Adult and Teenage Resources and Programs for Special Needs

As mentioned, the above programs for older children and adults are less focused on medical diagnosis and treatment because a prior diagnosis should have been accomplished earlier in a child's life. Indeed, a young adult may need ongoing treatment and medication for special needs or any number of other diagnoses. Depending on the diagnosis or diagnoses they may need ongoing follow up by a number of specialized medical professionals as well as any other programs available to help each person be as independent as possible. There are programs which can provide training with regard to the Life Skills mentioned previously where Activities of Daily Living are taught and reinforced to those who are delayed in physical or cognitive development. This is why it is important to discuss the concept of transition planning into adult services with someone in your sphere of schools and programs for people with disabilities or health care professionals. This is discussed in the chapter on Transition Planning for Children. You should also search locally for services for people with disabilities.

chapter eight

INDIVIDUALIZED EDUCATION PROGRAM AND 504 ACCOMODATIONS

I see many parents with children who have learning disabilities or special needs, who are frustrated because they are not getting the support they need from their schools. This can be a very helpless feeling because they are trying to grapple with a huge and overwhelming system they don't understand and don't have the training to deal with. If this is what you are experiencing, then you need to educate yourself regarding the following information and laws. The best way to get the most assistance from school for your children is to contact the agencies in your state who are there to help you with your special needs child. They can help educate you and, in some cases, they can actually go with you to the school to help you advocate for your child.

The following information is from federal law regarding the Individualized Education Program, 504 Accommodations and other related programs you should be aware of. There are organizations in most states who consult with parents to assist them with these and other programs for school age children. They are found by going to the U.S. Department of Education website at www.ed.gov, then search for Education Resource Organizations Directory and click on Organizations by Type, then click on State Parent Training and Information Center (Disabilities). The best way to find such a parent center in your state is by going to the National Parent Technical Assistance Center online at www.parentcenternetwork.org. These websites and other methods for finding them will change over time so your methods for finding them may need to change.

Knowing these laws and facts as well as where to go to receive training, consultation, and advocacy will give you power and confidence when working with the school system. I have been to workshops and seminars by the organization in my state and the information and help they provide is invaluable to parents with special needs children as well as professionals. Some of what you read from this point on is from that same parent education center, but the information is directly from federal law and applicable to parents navigating the school system in any state. If you are struggling with the school, contact the organizations above and get some help.

What is an Individualized Education Program or IEP

An Individualized Education Program is a plan that is put into place by a team of individuals who are working to provide the best educational experience for a special needs child. This team usually includes the parents, the special education teacher, the principal, therapists, or other school personnel. If your child has a special need then he or she should have in place an IEP or a 504 plan to maximize his or her potential in school. A 504 plan is for a child who does not qualify for an IEP but does need educational accommodations to assist in the learning process. An example of a 504 accommodation would be to move a child with poor eye sight to the front row of a classroom so he or she is better able to see the chalkboard or whiteboard.

Individualized Education Program (IEP) Tips for Parents

EVALUATION

- Making a Referral and Request for Initial Evaluation:
- Ask in writing for evaluation; keep a copy of your request.
- Explain the child's problem(s) and why the evaluation is needed.
- Parental consent is required for evaluation.
- Keep the letter to one (1) page and use bullet points.
- Parents have the right to an Independent Educational Evaluation of the student if they disagree with the school's evaluation.

Evaluation Questions to Ask:
- What is the test measuring?
- What is the average or normal on this test?
- Where is my child in comparison to the normal?
- What does this mean in terms of teaching my child?

ELIGIBILITY

Based off of assessments and IEP team input.

Student must meet one of the 13 classifications and require specialized instruction. (See IEP Handbook for more information.)

PREPARATION FOR THE IEP MEETING

IEP Meeting Preparation:
- Gather information to share: medical, psychological, other assessments.
- Keep a file of all important information related to your child's educational record.
- Review your child's school records and current IEP if there is one.
- List what you see as your child's strengths and needs.
- Write down your priorities and long range goals for your child.
- List services that you believe your child needs to attain the goals you have identified.
- Write down your questions.
- Communicate with your team prior to the meeting:
- Ask for and review evaluation data.
- Share your ideas for IEP goals with the team.
- Ask to see a draft of the IEP goals prior to the team meeting.
- Inviting Individuals to the IEP Meeting:
- Parents may invite anyone who will be helpful to the IEP meeting.
- It is appropriate to inform the school who you are inviting prior to the meeting.
- Students are encouraged to participate in the IEP meeting where appropriate.
- Key members of the IEP Team: Parent(s), LEA (Local Education Agency), Special Education Teacher, General Education Teacher.

Individualized Education Programs and 504 Accommodations

PARTICIPATION IN THE IEP MEETING

- Use good communication skills throughout the meeting.
- LEA representative should conduct the meeting.
- Have IEP team members introduce themselves and their roles.
- Parents must be given a copy of Utah's **Procedural Safeguards Notice** outlining specific parent rights under IDEA.
- Make sure the concerns about your child as well as the child's strengths are listed on the IEP.
- Communicate your priorities and suggestions for goals. Consider how they fit with the goals proposed by the rest of the team.
- Be prepared to negotiate. See if there are alternative ways to meet goals.
- Ask for clarification of any information or statements that are unclear to you.

What Your Signature Means:

- All participants should sign the IEP.
- All signatures on the IEP show participation and attendance.
- Parents may note on the IEP that they "disagree" or have concerns.

FOLLOW-UP ON THE IEP MEETING

- Express appreciation for the efforts of school personnel.

- Monitor your child's progress.

- Know how often progress reports will be sent home and know how best to communicate with the IEP team.

- The IEP can be changed as needed.

- Parents may request an IEP meeting if there are concerns or problems with the IEP or if the child is not making satisfactory progress.

- IEP teams are to meet annually.

PROBLEM SOLVING IN THE IEP PROCESS

Proceed thoughtfully! Seek to resolve difficulties at the lowest possible level.

When It Just Doesn't Work:

- Communicate with your school team.

- Follow the chain of command which is typically:

- Teacher

- Principal

- School District Special Education Director/Supervisor

- Utah State Office of Education, Special Education

All provisions of the Individuals with Disabilities Education Act (IDEA 2004) also apply to Charter Schools.

For more detailed information see the Utah Parent Center's "Parents as Partners in the IEP Process" handbook at www.utahparentcenter.org/publications/handbooks

IDEA Act of 2004

This next section is somewhat technical but it needs to be in this chapter to help parents who have children with disabilities understand their rights.

INDIVIDUALS WITH DISABILITIES EDUCATION IMPROVEMENT ACT 2004[3]

Commonly referred to as IDEA 2004
IDEA Reauthorized–H.R. 1350

The Individuals with Disabilities Education Act (IDEA) is a law that ensures services to children with disabilities throughout the nation. IDEA governs how states and public agencies provide early intervention, special education, and related services to eligible infants, toddlers, children, and youth with disabilities.

SIX IMPORTANT PRINCIPLES COVERED IN IDEA 2004

The following six important principles covered in IDEA are key to understanding the intent and spirit of the law. These principles include:

1. Free appropriate public education (FAPE): The right to FAPE means special education and related services are available to eligible children with disabilities age three to 22 and are to be provided at no cost to the parents. The specially designed educational programs and services reflect the child's individual educational needs and are to be provided in conformity with the Individualized Educational Program (IEP). The provision of FAPE differs for each child, but the principle is the same. FAPE applies to all qualifying children with disabilities, including those who have been suspended or expelled from school.

---

3   *Individuals with Disabilities Education Improvement Act (2004). Retrieved from http://idea.ed.gov/download/statute.html.*

2. Appropriate evaluation: An appropriate evaluation gathers accurate information to determine eligibility or continued eligibility; it also identifies the student's strengths and educational needs. An individualized education program is then designed to respond to the student's needs.

3. Individualized Education Program (IEP): The IEP is a legally binding, written document that outlines the special education program, services, and related services based on the child's educational needs.

4. Least restrictive environment (LRE): The LRE is the environment where the student can receive an appropriate education designed to meet his or her special education needs, while still being educated with nondisabled peers to the maximum extent appropriate.

5. Parent and student participation in decision making: IDEA requires that parents must be given the opportunity to play a central role in the planning and decision making regarding their child's education. Parents must have the opportunity to participate in the meetings regarding identification, evaluation, educational placement, and the provision of FAPE to the student. Student rights and participation are strongly encouraged, particularly when addressing transition planning.

6. Procedural due process: The guarantee of procedural due process means that there are safeguards designed to protect the rights of the parents and their children with disabilities, as well as to give families and schools a mechanism for resolving disputes.

EARLY INTERVENTION

Infants and toddlers with disabilities (birth-2) and their families receive early intervention services under Part C of IDEA. Services for this age group are called Early Intervention. Early Intervention services are family-centered, multidisciplinary, comprehensive and community-based and honor the values and beliefs of the family. The specific early intervention services for a child are written in an **Individualized Family Service Plan (IFSP)** which is based on the concerns and priorities of the family.

The Early Intervention program must conduct transition planning to move eligible children from early intervention to preschool programs. This planning for the transition to preschool should be implemented at least 90 calendar days before the child turns three and is eligible for the preschool program. An IEP should be implemented by the child's 3rd birthday. Parents are to be involved in these team planning processes.

SPECIAL EDUCATION

Part B of IDEA 2004 outlines the special education process which is available for eligible students with disabilities from age three through graduation or to age 22, including special education preschool which serves children ages three to five. (Your State Office of Education will most likely be the lead agency responsible for overseeing special education.) A specific child's educational needs and services are written in an Individualized Education Program or IEP.

PARENT RIGHTS SUMMARY

- Parents have the right to provide information and be involved in the evaluation process. Parents can be involved in the review of existing evaluation data during the initial evaluation and re-evaluation of their child.

- Parents have the right to be a part of the group that makes the decision regarding their child's educational placement.

- Parents must be given the opportunity to participate in meetings held with respect to the identification, evaluation, and educational placement of their child, and the provision of FAPE to their child. School personnel may have informal meetings without the parents.

- Parents have the right to receive periodic reports on the progress the child is making toward meeting the annual goals such as through the use of quarterly or other periodic reports at the time report cards are issued.

STUDENT RIGHTS

- Students must be invited to attend the IEP meeting if a purpose of the meeting will be the consideration of the post-secondary goals and the transition services needed to assist the student in reaching those goals which are based on individual student needs, preferences, and interests. If the student does not attend the IEP meeting, the team must take other steps to ensure that the student's preferences and interests are considered (§300.321).

- Transition planning will begin for the student with disabilities beginning no later than the first IEP to be in effect when the student turns 16 (the IEP meeting conducted when the student is 15 years old), or younger if determined appropriate by the IEP Team. For more information, please see the section in this book on transition planning (§300.322).

- On the student's 18th birthday, parental rights transfer to the student. At least one year before the student's 18th birthday, a statement is required on the student's IEP, that the student and parents have been informed of the transfer of rights (except for a student who has been determined to be incompetent by a court). Parents may want to consider guardianship options, at least for educational programming, if they believe the student does not have the ability to provide **informed consent** about educational decisions. Otherwise, parental rights will transfer to the student. (§300.320)

Eligible students at all public schools including charter schools have the right to FAPE (free appropriate public education). §300.320

Children who are placed in the private schools by their parents do not have an individual right to receive some or all of the special education and related services that the student would receive if enrolled in a public school. There are, however, requirements for the school district where the private school is located to locate, identify, and evaluate students with disabilities enrolled in the private school.

The LEA must develop and implement a services plan and provide some funding for each student that has been designated to receive services."

504 Accommodation

As referred to above, if your child does not qualify for an IEP he or she may be able to receive an accommodation in the school setting under federal antidiscrimination law. This following information is from the same organization referred to in this chapter whose mandate it is to educate the public regarding issues with special needs children and adults in employment, programs accessibility, and schools.

Craig T. Mitchell, LCSW

"SECTION 504 OF THE REHABILITATION ACT[4]

An Antidiscrimination Law

With the passage of the Rehabilitation Act of 1973, Congress required that federal fund recipients make their programs and activities accessible to all individuals with disabilities. The law states that, 'No qualified individual with disabilities, shall, solely by reason of her or his disability be excluded from the participation in, be denied the benefits of, or be subjected to discrimination under any program or activity receiving federal financial assistance.'

Section 504 protects persons from discrimination based upon their disability status

A person has a disability within the definition for Section 504 if he or she:

- Has a mental or physical impairment which substantially limits one or more of such person's major life activities;

- Has a record of such impairments; or

- Is regarded as having such an impairment.

Major Life Activities

Major life activities include functions such as:

- Caring for oneself
- Performing manual tasks
- Seeing
- Hearing
- Eating
- Sleeping
- Walking
- Standing
- Lifting
- Non-volitional bodily functions
- Speaking
- Breathing
- Learning
- Reading
- Concentrating
- Thinking
- Communicating
- Working, and
- Bending

---

[4] *Section 504, Rehabilitation Act* (1973). Retrieved from http://www.dol.gov/oasam/regs/statutes/sec504.htm.

When a condition does not substantially limit a major life activity, the individual does not qualify under Section 504.

Section 504 has three major areas of emphasis: employment, program accessibility, and requirements for preschool, elementary, and secondary education. All students in special education are protected by Section 504. Section 504 regulations cover a larger group of students with disabilities than are in special education. Some examples of disabilities that could be covered include:

- Attention deficit disorder (ADD)
- Attention deficit hyperactivity disorder (ADHD)
- Learning Disabilities
- Cancer
- Asthma
- Special Health Care Needs
- Parents with hearing impairments who need an interpreter
- Homebound students requiring services for when the disability substantially limits a major life activity.

Although Section 504 does not require school districts to develop an individualized plan with annual goals and objectives, it is recommended that the school document the services and/or accommodations that are provided for each eligible Section 504 student in a written plan. If a student requires 504 accommodations, a team must meet to develop a plan that outlines the student's services and accommodations. Parent and student participation should always be encouraged. The quality of educational services provided to students with disabilities must be the equivalent to the services provided to students without disabilities.

If the student qualifies under Section 504, accommodations could be written in a Section 504 plan. Parents may request a Section 504 evaluation if they believe the child qualifies under Section 504, or the child did not qualify for special education.

A few more laws you need to be aware of if your child struggles in school:

FAMILY EDUCATION RIGHTS AND PRIVACY ACT

FERPA or the Buckley Amendment
The Family Education Rights and Privacy Act of 1974 (P.L. 93-380, FERPA), also known as the Buckley Amendment:

- Guarantees you the right to inspect and review your child's file. You also have the right to receive copies of the file information.

- Says that only people who need to see the file can see it.

- Allows you to challenge information in the file you feel is inaccurate or misleading.

- Allows you to ask the school to remove something in the file that you disagree with. If the request is denied, you have at least two options:

- You may attach a statement to the page in question telling why you disagree.

- You may request a hearing (However, consider the value of this formal process and what you need to accomplish).

THE MCKINNEY-VENTO ACT (TITLE X, PART C OF NO CHILD LEFT BEHIND)

The McKinney-Vento Act, which later became part of the No Child Left Behind Act (NCLB), mandates protections and services for children and youth who are homeless including those with disabilities.

The 2004 reauthorization of IDEA also includes amendments that reinforce timely assessment, inclusion, and continuity of services for homeless children and youth who have disabilities. The following are a few of the provisions.

Who is considered homeless?

Anyone who lacks a fixed, regular, and adequate nighttime residence including:

- Sharing the housing of others due to lack of housing, economic hardship, or similar reason
- Living in motels, hotels, trailer parks, camping grounds, due to lack of adequate alternative accommodations
- Living in emergency or transitional shelters
- Abandoned in hospitals
- Awaiting foster care placement
- Living in a public or private place not designed for humans to live
- Living in cars, parks, abandoned buildings, public train stations, etc.
- A migrant child who qualifies under any of the above

The Educational Rights for Children and Youth Experiencing Homelessness

The following are considered educational rights for homeless children/youth:

- Right to a homeless education liaison in every public school district
- Right to immediate enrollment in school where seeking enrollment without proof of residency, immunizations, school records, or other documents
- Right to choose among the local school where they are living, the school they attended before they lost their housing, or the school where they were last enrolled

- Right to transportation to their school of origin

- Right to be free from harassment and exclusion. Segregation based on a student's status and homelessness is strictly prohibited.

- Right to access to educational services for which they are eligible including IDEA services, ESL, gifted and talented programs, vocational/technical education, and school nutrition programs.

- Right to be notified of their options and rights under McKinney-Vento. Liaisons must post rights of students experiencing homelessness in schools and other places in the community.

- Right to have disagreements with the school settled quickly.

Note:

The previous pages provided an overview of several laws which protect individuals with disabilities including the Individuals with Disabilities Education Act (IDEA).

IDEA 2004 requires that the school keep copies of school records if not having copies would prevent the parent from inspecting and reviewing those records. §300.613"

The above information was found in publications from the Utah Parent Center website[5] and Parents as Partners in the IEP Process Parent Handbook.[6] For more information go to the U.S. Department of Education, **A Guide to the Individualized Education Program.**

---

5   Utah Parent Center (2011). Retrieved from https://www.utahparentcenter.org/.

6   Utah Parent Center (2011). *Parents as partners in the IEP process.* Retrieved from http://www.utahparentcenter.org/wp-content/uploads/2014/07/Parents-as-Partners-in-the-IEP-Process-Handbook.pdf.

chapter nine
SIBLINGS OF CHILDREN WITH SPECIAL NEEDS

I have been around special needs children for over 30 years. They have been in my home as my wife provided respite care for them. We were licensed as a foster home to provide these services to them and their families. I have also worked at an agency for over 23 years which serves children with special health care needs. In all this time and with all this exposure to these children and families, I had not fully understood the degree to which siblings of special needs children are impacted by their special needs siblings. I have seen many of these kids come to our clinics with their parents to help take care of their special need siblings, and I have been impressed by how patient and helpful they are with them. In 2010, I was given the invitation to attend what is called a Sibshop Training with the creator of Sibshops, Don Meyer.

I learned that siblings of children who have special needs have many of their own needs and concerns. Common among these siblings are feelings that range from being proud of their special needs brothers and sisters to being embarrassed by them. Don Meyer has created an environment in which these children, from the ages of 8 to 13, can openly share how they feel without feeling guilty or judged. It was amazing to see how these kids were so very responsible and caring toward their brothers and sisters, and in this environment they were able to express their own issues they deal with.

The most surprising insight to me was that by the time they are in their early teens these very caring siblings understand that they, especially the older or oldest siblings, will someday become the primary caretaker of their special needs brother or sister. This has direct impact on their entire direction in life. To begin with, they will only date those who are not put off by their special needs sibling. If that person is understanding and accepting of the special needs sibling, he or she will be much more likely to advance the relationship. These siblings will also decide on careers and degrees that will allow them to remain in the same area and be involved in the lives of their families. They will also make decisions about their homes, knowing they will probably have their special needs sibling living with them after their parents are unable to take care of them. This can also impact the number of children they have in their own family. One can only imagine the heavy responsibility some of these kids feel toward their siblings and parents.

What is a Sibshop

A Sibshop consists of putting children from 8 to 13 years of age in same age groups and starting off by making funny nametags and playing a number of games requiring them to move about, all the while having a great deal of fun. This is followed by the leader sitting down on the floor with them and discussing strengths and weaknesses. They are given a pencil and paper and paired off with another child they don't know. They question each other about these strengths and weaknesses for themselves and their brothers and sisters with special needs. This is called an interview. When this is completed, they meet back together and introduce their partners and tell the group the partner's strengths and weaknesses and about their special needs siblings. These children begin to understand that they have a lot of company regarding the way they feel. It becomes a safe place to share and feel okay about how they feel. This is just the beginning of many other lively and insightful games and activities. The Sibshop lasts four hours, and in this timeframe these kids really discover themselves, their siblings, and others who have similar experiences to a depth that is very insightful. They learn about their common joys and concerns they share with other siblings. They learn how others handle their own situations and the implications of having a sibling with special needs.

Adult Siblings of Special Needs Brothers and Sisters

During this training a panel of six adults who had siblings with special needs was conducted. One of these individuals was the sister of the young woman who spent quite a bit of time in my home in respite care. I had met her before and therefore her words had deeper meaning for me. I was awestruck as she told us about when she was about 12 or 13 and she realized that someday she would be the primary caretaker of her sister. She accepted this without hesitation or resentment and certainly without begrudging the monumental task in her future. She had a desire to go into a certain field of study in college, but when she found that she would have to go away to pursue her education she changed her major so she could stay close by and assist her mother with her sister. She made a decision early on that whoever she married would have to be completely comfortable with her sister. Some suitors were not suitable, pun intended. The first time her eventual husband entered her home, her sister ran naked in front of him with her mother in pursuit. She was apologetic, and he responded that it didn't bother him and was "no big deal." From the very start of their relationship the issue of her sister was out on the table, and it became a nonissue. A few years ago she and her husband built a new home complete with an apartment to someday provide a place for her sister. This was a striking disclosure which was made all the more remarkable when the rest of the panel told very similar stories. We have a whole subculture of individuals in our midst who have siblings with special needs, and we have no idea the burdens and responsibilities they carry for most of their lives. From what the panel of siblings described, they do not consider what they do for their siblings as a burden. They just do what they have always done, and I salute them.

Issues These Siblings May Face

- Burnout from taking care of their sibling
- Excessive expectations from their parents to help with their sibling
- Long-term stress about being there and supporting their parents.
- Guilt about not doing enough
- Embarrassment about having a sibling with special needs
- Isolation from others because they have a sibling with special needs
- Frustration about their circumstances
- Jealousy of the attention their sibling receives from their parents and others
- Resentment for the attention their sibling receives from their parents and others
- Money may be less available because family resources are used for the special needs child
- Fear of the responsibilities they face in the future
- Over identification with the special needs sibling i.e. Am I going to have autism, etc?
- Worrying about the future
- Opportunities These Siblings May Enjoy
- Attending Special Olympics with their sibling
- Opportunities to experience special needs organizations
- Understanding how people are all different and unique
- Learning how to advocate for people who have needs
- Developing compassion and empathy

- Learning patience
- Appreciating their own health and blessings
- Enjoying and experiencing some of the perks their siblings receive
- Developing maturity
- Gaining insights about life, which others will never quite understand
- Pride in and love of their sibling is a special gift
- Tolerance of others
- Knowledge and wisdom growing out of their experiences with their sibling
- Increased personal strength

Sibs Informational Needs

Don Meyer points out important information siblings and parents need to understand. What is my sibling's disability and how do I describe it to others? I.e. cerebral palsy, downs syndrome, autism, etc. Parents need to provide information to all their children and even ask for doctors and providers to help educate their children. Parents need to plan ahead for their disabled child to minimize the responsibility siblings may experience. Then they need to make these plans known to their children. Parents can tell their children that they are preparing their special needs child to be as independent as possible, reassuring their siblings that this is what they hope to have in place. There are a variety of ways siblings can be lovingly involved without having to be full caretakers.

Mr. Meyer recommends that parents let their kids be apart for a while until the siblings get through their embarrassment, especially when they are in junior high and high school. He has also discovered that siblings often believe their special needs siblings can do a lot more than their parents require them to do.

For more information about how to start a Sibshop, contact the Sibling Support Project at (206) 297-6368 or donmeyer@siblingsupport.org. The website is www.siblingsupport.org. If you are an adult and you would like to have contact with other adult sibs in your area then visit this website and get started.

chapter ten
WHAT ARE OUR ATTITUDES ABOUT FAMILY PROBLEMS AND SPECIAL NEEDS

What Are Our Attitudes about Our Family Problems?

Most of us don't want to believe we have any needs at all, even if our world is falling apart all around us. I see marriage relationships struggling with arguments, misunderstanding, lack of communication, or children having difficulties in school socially, with math, reading, or other subjects. Other children are distracted or have learning disabilities, and some parents avoid dealing with these issues because they are so busy themselves. They don't want to believe their child has problems, thinking he or she will adapt. Divorce can cause so much heartache and collateral damage with children and parents that everyone is just getting by, trying to ignore all the issues. Some children are abused emotionally, physically, or sexually. If these issues are not addressed, worked through, and resolved, they will be carried along into adulthood with further consequences occurring in their own families and other environments.

Unfortunately, pride or just stubborn attitudes keep us from asking for help, even if we know who to ask. Of the people you know how many have, at one time or other, been in need of some kind of help mentally or emotionally? How many of these people have actually been to a counselor? Probably very few and the majority who do get professional help will be women. Thank goodness for women and mothers who look for answers and actively seek for those who can assist them and their children.

There are certain people who are very strong and resilient who seem to handle almost any challenge they are given in life, and they do so without needing much input from others. There are such people among us, but even they, at times, need a little guidance or someone to open up to.

What Are Our Attitudes about Children's Special Needs?

Parents who don't seek help for their children early on become painfully aware over time that they should have intervened and sought out a diagnosis and treatment. By this time, in some cases, it may be too late to make substantial changes in the early development of the child. These folks believe (somewhat naively) their child will be just fine developmentally or academically because he or she just needed a little more time to mature. They can't entertain the thought that something might not be right with their child. I see more of this with fathers who have a denial system that stubbornly keeps them from seeing the truth. Some of these fathers even make it difficult or impossible for the mothers to initiate intervention for fear they will go against his wishes. If they go ahead and make an appointment for an assessment they take the chance of facing some form of retribution from him in the form of ridicule or even abuse.

No Guilt Parenting and Seeking Resources for Our Family

I am not trying to guilt parents or individuals into taking action. I would like to create a no guilt approach to caring for our families. If we can educate ourselves enough to know where to go and what questions to ask, we can make our families better developed, capable, and healthy. In this current economy, services and programs are becoming scarce around us. Networking with those who have some local knowledge about resources can make all the difference in finding help. I hope to cultivate an awareness of resources in your locality. In some areas of the world there are few places to go when we have needs whether mental, emotional, physical, spiritual, or medical. Other, more populated places, have much more than we might imagine to address these needs. If we can learn how and where to search we might be able to find understanding people, professionals, and programs with just the helping hand we need.

Fathers, Step Up to the Plate. You Have a Responsibility to Your Family

I want to talk to fathers here because you have a great deal of influence with and a responsibility for your family. In many cases, you have the financial resources and may even control the family finances. Without your direct support your children may not be able to reach their true potential. If they are delayed in any area of development, what is the harm if they get some tutoring one-on-one? Maybe some speech therapy will help them communicate better and produce more self-confidence. Wouldn't you want that for your child? Help with reading can make a huge difference in a child's life. If you will think back as a child, was there ever a time when you were embarrassed about reading or some other subject you had problems with in school? If not, do you recall seeing another student in such a situation? Do you really want any child of yours to struggle and feel like he or she is stupid or dumb? Those are harsh words but you know how school children are very willing to call someone stupid or dumb. All it takes is being told this just once to start a lifetime of self-doubt and emotional pain. Don't take any chances with your children. You are their protector and provider so step up and do what needs to be done. If you have any feedback or information that your children might be behind or that they might have some mental-emotional problems, be the protector and provide them with anything they might need. Many parents will provide all kinds of gifts, going all out to try and make Christmas and birthdays special for their children. They will also provide them the best medical attention when they are sick. But when it comes to these other important issues affecting development, self-esteem, and being a whole, complete, and acceptable person, some parents hesitate and do not act. Please don't let pride get in the way of making sure your child gets the very best, especially early in his or her development.

chapter eleven

ORGANIZATIONS AND FOUNDATIONS FOR RARE DISORDERS

Foundations for Rare Disorders

There are numerous organizations called foundations which have been created by concerned people from the medical profession, philanthropists, and even parents who join together to disseminate information and educate the public regarding new developments and treatments for rare disorders. The largest organization I am aware of is called NORD, the National Organization for Rare Disorders. They have a very extensive website at www.rarediseases.org. They have information on over 1,200 rare diseases and provide direction to network with organizations and individuals who have similar diseases and problems. They also have information about new research, new medications, and newsletters to inform the public about news-worthy items. They even offer help and advice to help you create your own organization or how to grow one you may have already started. They also give information related to advocating for rare diseases whether it is to change federal, state, or local laws. They can connect you with organizations that are already advocating and leading the way to educate and improve the lives of families who are living with rare disorders. They have an excellent website, and I encourage you to visit it and learn more.

There are several other organizations with websites who distribute information about specific disorders. If you have a diagnosis or suspect your family member may have a diagnosis, then search the internet and see if you can identify an organization that has been created to help you know more about it. A good example of such an organization is the Epilepsy Foundation. I used to run a support group for parents who have children with epilepsy. I ordered books, children's books, pamphlets, charts, and much more to provide educational information for this group. Regardless of what you're looking for you will probably find information on it when you search the internet.

chapter twelve

BE CAREFUL WHEN RESEARCHING AND APPLYING DIAGNOSTIC SYMPTOMS TO YOUR FAMILY MEMBER

I do have one caution about getting information on the Internet or elsewhere. Sometimes parents look at symptoms, and they become convinced that their child has that disease or diagnosis. I have seen a lot of this over the years, and I caution you to be very careful. Sometimes these parents will come into the doctor and they want a confirmation that their child has a certain diagnosis only to have the doctor indicate, for various reasons, that the diagnosis they are settled on is inaccurate. Some of these people take offense and argue or attempt to defend their belief, even to the point of becoming very upset. I recommend to anyone who researches symptoms of disorders and diseases that they do so carefully without buying into what they find until they get at least two professional opinions.

I attended a seminar for psychotherapists regarding diagnosing and treating clients. A presentation was given cautioning us, as therapists, to be aware of the tendency of going to a seminar and learning about a diagnosis and then returning to our offices and diagnosing many of our patients with what we have just learned. I have noticed this in my own practice that I can get caught up in learning more about a diagnosis or treatment, and I need to be cautious not to see the same symptoms in my patients. The message here is to be careful how you apply what you learn during your research.

I have seen parents argue with doctors because they are convinced that their child has a certain diagnosis. I have also seen knowledgeable parents present convincing evidence enough to lean a doctor to consider and then provide a diagnosis that otherwise may have gone in a different direction. My recommendation is to use balance and ask direct questions if you have a belief that your family member might be suffering from a certain kind of problem. Present your evidence, but at the same time be open to considering what the doctor says. You can always go to someone else and ask for a second opinion.

chapter thirteen
SOME SUGGESTIONS WHEN YOU HAVE A CHILD WITH A SPECIAL NEED

If you have a child you think might have a special need, it would be well for you to read the chapter in this book "IDENTIFYING NORMAL AND DELAYED DEVELOPMENT IN CHILDREN." You would also benefit from going to a website that helps families identify resources for children with disabilities called the National Dissemination Center for Children with Disabilities. The website is http://nichcy.org. You will find information on what a disability is, topics regarding disabilities, publications, state and national organizations, baby and toddler programs, programs for children from 3 to 22 years of age, disability and education laws, research, and much more. Some state organizations provide assessments for children, and others only refer families to facilities that diagnose and possibly treat disabilities. In some locations special needs staff travel (sponsored by the state or private medical organizations) to remote places to diagnose and possibly to provide some treatment. In other states or locations families have to travel to receive medical services. If you are fortunate enough to live close to major hospitals, you will find it easier to identify where you need to go for evaluations and treatment.

Children's Hospitals

There are a number of children's hospitals who diagnose and treat children whether the parents can afford to pay or not. Your primary care physician can help you determine if there is such a facility locally or where the closest one is located. A very good example of such a hospital is Shriners Hospital. Shriners Hospitals are located across the country and are completely free of charge to families. They bill insurances, but they do not bill families. There is a process to go through when applying but don't be intimidated because you will be guided along the way when you contact one of their hospitals. The website for Shriners Hospitals is www.shrinershospitalsforchildren.org. The phone number for patient referrals and eligibility is 800-237-5055 in the U.S. and 800-361-7256 in Canada. This hospital system treats children with orthopedic needs (muscles and bones), burn care, cleft lip and palate, and spinal cord injury. All of these services may not be available at each of their hospitals, however if families can travel to other locations they will be served.

Neonatal Follow-Up Program or NFP

The Neonatal Follow-up Program is a nationwide program to follow the progress of infants who have been born prematurely or have other severe birth problems. These infants usually spend as many weeks in the newborn intensive care units of hospitals as they are premature, some for several months. The NFP program I am involved with has a team consisting of developmental pediatricians, psychologists, occupational/ physical therapists, nurses, a neurologist, ophthalmologist (eye doctor), speech pathologist, audiologist, dietician, and me, the social worker. Each time these children come to a clinic they are evaluated regarding their progress and, if necessary, I refer them to local programs such as the early intervention program or others. This is a very helpful program to help parents understand what is going on with their children who are at risk for diverse problems. Parents can ask questions and become more educated regarding how their child is doing. These children are followed up to four and a half years of age depending on what their diagnoses are. Data is collected and sent to government programs in order to determine the effectiveness of current treatments in the neonatal intensive care units of hospitals as well as other useful statistics. If you have a new premature infant you may want to ask the hospital staff if there is a Neonatal Follow-up Program in your area to follow your child's progress.

Orofacial or Craniofacial Team

If you have a child with a cleft lip or palate or similar diagnosis, you should look for a program in your area that has what is referred to as an orofacial or craniofacial team. This means your child would be evaluated by a team of specialists on the same day. I have been a part of many of these teams, and it is a very convenient and thorough way of evaluating all the needs of the child. The team I am referring to included: a plastic surgeon, an ear nose and throat doctor, an orthodontist, a speech pathologist, an audiologist, a nutritionist or dietician, a nurse and me, the social worker. The advantage of the team concept is that the child is able to see all the specialists at the clinic on the same day instead of going to them separately and hoping they will communicate with each other to coordinate all the procedures he or she requires. After seeing all the patients on the day of the clinic, the team has a staff meeting to discuss each child and what needs to be done in each case. After hearing from every specialist on the team, decisions are made to treat and schedule certain procedures or therapies or to wait for more growth and development according to the child's needs. The nurse and/or secretary then contacts the families to inform them of the team's recommendations. Notes from the team are also sent to the families and the primary care physician as requested by the parents.

Respite Care

If you are unfamiliar with what respite care is please read the chapter on RESPITE CARE. There is information regarding how to find respite care programs locally. I encourage all the parents I work with who have family members with special needs to apply for respite care programs. Where I live it takes quite a while to receive respite care after applying, so I hope you will seek out a program now because by the time you get funded you will most likely be in need of a break from the care of a special needs child. I ask you to not feel guilty about this because everyone needs to get away from the stress and care of children whether they have special needs or not. It is simply a fact. You are more than a machine and even machines need to be turned off and serviced on a regular basis, so take your turn because it will revitalize you and give you more energy.

SSI

SSI is a program for people with disabilities and is operated through the Social Security Administration. SSI stands for Supplemental Security Income. To qualify, one has to be diagnosed with a severe disability and the family income has to fall within certain income guidelines. If you have a child with a special need, and you believe it is severe enough then I would suggest you apply for this program. A child who receives SSI will receive a monthly check and, in most cases, he or she will qualify for Medicaid as well. The amount the family receives depends on the number of children in the home and the monthly family income. You can apply online through the Social Security website or call 1-800-772-1213. When you call make sure you have the following information:

- The child's name and social security number.

- The child's diagnosis or diagnoses, the more severe the more likely he or she will qualify.

- Proof of income for the past two months.

Medicaid

Medicaid is a federal program that is administered through each state. It is medical insurance that can take care of many of the needs of a special needs child. In most places it is in effect until the child turns either 18 or 19, depending on the program he or she is on. When looking to apply for Medicaid you should search for a Medicaid office in your community. In my experience most children with special needs from lower to middle incomes are on Medicaid. It is a critical program to have for a child with a special need because it can provide much needed medical services for that child.

NORD

NORD is the acronym for the National Organization for Rare Diseases. This is a very helpful website for families with special needs because it has a wealth of information on rare diseases. Their library is large, and you will be able to connect with organizations which have been created to help families who have members with these diseases. These organizations are called foundations, and they exist to inform the public on the latest news, research, and conferences related to such rare diseases. The website for NORD is www.rarediseases.org.

chapter forteen
RESPITE CARE

What is Respite Care?

Respite Care a Very Critical Need with Few Resources

One of the greatest needs I see currently, which is being chopped out of many state budgets, is respite care. What is respite care? Respite care is the temporary care of someone with special needs by others while the primary caretakers such as family members take a break. This can be with licensed foster families, licensed facilities, family members or trusted friends depending on the regulations in each state. These programs have been funded by states in the past to avoid placing the special needs individual in some type of institutional care facility. This could be for a child or adult who has a severe diagnosis who cannot care for himself or herself and needs ongoing supervision. I have seen countless people over the years that could really use respite care to provide a break from the constant care of a loved one. The curious thing which I run into often is that these caretakers do not want anyone else to care for their loved ones because they feel guilty letting anyone else take over for them, even for a few hours. They are resolved that no one can do as good a job, and they are offended if I suggest they consider utilizing such a program. Many of these people say they have a caring family who helps, and they can do it on their own. This is wonderful yet I fear that in a lot of cases the mother or the main care giver becomes burned out and tries desperately to not let on that he or she really needs help. They don't want anyone else involved because of the belief that no one could ever take care of their child like they can, and they are correct. However, others can do a good job of caring for the child or adult for short periods of time.

My Personal Experience with Respite Care

There is a couple who are very close friends of mine, who have I have known since we were young. He is a social worker named Dennis; his wife, Joyce, is a registered nurse. They have written a number of books on the subject of grief. They are particularly experienced and suited for this task for several reasons. His mother committed suicide; her father died of a heart attack in the early morning on Christmas day. Their first child was stillborn, and their third child was born with cerebral palsy. I will refer to them in Book 1 on the chapter dealing with GRIEF. I believe we were brought together for a number of reasons, including this book, so that my wife and I would be introduced to the world of children with special needs. All the knowledge and credit here goes to my wife, Arlette, because she was completely dedicated to these amazing children and parents. I was basically along for the ride, all the while learning from her and her "kids," as she called them.

In 1979 Dennis moved to California to begin his career after he received his Master's degree. Two years later I finished my Master's degree and went to work in Washington state. About three years later Dennis was transferred to my office to become the director. A few years later, as my wife was talking to Joyce, they decided that Arlette would start to do some respite care for them by taking care of their son Cameron who had cerebral palsy. This is a very serious condition which, in severe cases, robs a person of the ability to walk, talk, and control movements of his or her arms and legs. These people are usually in a wheelchair and require 24 hour-per-day care for almost all their needs. When given the chance, Arlette jumped at it, and we found ourselves in the middle of being licensed as foster parents. This is something we were involved in until 2010. I say we but I really mean my wife because she did all the work and care for these children and later with adults who would come into our home. I would provide some of the muscle (I use that term loosely) to lift the kids from bed, bath, or wheelchair when she needed additional help or to chase a child down who was a runner. Our own children became savvy and very comfortable around children with special health care needs also. Our kids were and still are wonderful with these individuals and they are competent in providing care for those with special needs.

After we were licensed by the state, Arlette started taking Cameron on various occasions while Dennis and Joyce got away for a few hours at a time. She discovered she loved doing this so much that she became a real expert in all kinds of skills like inserting feeding tubes, administration of medications, oxygen, and bed sore management. She became adept at knowing seizures, suctioning a child's throat, and going with the biological parents to see doctors and giving feedback to them as important medical decisions were made. She learned to do physical, occupational and speech therapy exercises as assigned by licensed therapists. This was perfect for her because she could work with these kids in our home while being a mother to our children. She was amazing, loving every minute of what she did. I won't call it her job because it was more to her than that; it was selfless service.

Over time, she began to pick up more clients because the caseworker recognized how dedicated and competent she was. I remember coming home one day after work and there were three kids there with special needs; two of which were there waiting for their parents to pick them up after work. She had approximately 10 to 12 kids who were regulars that were in and out of our home from a few hours at a time to a day or weekend to a week or so while their parents got away to recharge their batteries, so to speak. When they came to pick their children up they were so full of gratitude for the time away without having to worry about their child. They had a tremendous amount of trust in Arlette for her loving care.

When we moved away from Washington, the parents of the children Arlette served had a difficult time because they loved her so much and appreciated how she loved their children. She continued to receive cards, gifts, pictures, and letters years later from these grateful parents. Arlette had a very hard time as well because she really loved those children and their parents; there was an incredible bond between them.

This is what can happen when people are giving service and caring for others. One might say that in my wife's case she was getting paid so it was just a job. She would get around $30 to $35 per 24-hour period, so when you figure an hourly wage it is quite insignificant. She was up many times at night with these children because they had many needs requiring care almost like what a nurse would provide in a hospital.

More on Respite Care Services

Respite Care is a concept which has been around for many years. As mentioned, respite care can extend from providing care for a few hours to weekends or a week or two for family vacations. This care can be provided in the family home or at the home or facility of the provider. It can be a tremendous help to give the family something to look forward to, and gives them a break from the everyday, ongoing care which can be very taxing over time.

I know that to some families this concept seems selfish and uncaring. However, I have seen enough parents and siblings who have become burned out over many years of care. This is not because they are not totally committed and loving; it is because we, as human beings, cannot go on day after day, indefinitely, without getting breaks now and then. Think of it this way; during a regular 8-hour workday most people get two 15 minute breaks and a lunch break. How many breaks does a parent with a disabled child get in any week? The answer is very little, if any at all. Everyone needs to get away and have a diversion from work and stress, and believe me taking care of a child or an adult with a disability involves work and stress without exception. As much as you love your child, sibling, parent, spouse, etc. you have your limitations and need to recharge your batteries. Your cell phone can't continue working without being plugged in to receive new energy and neither can you. You're not a robot, and I ask that you consider very carefully what I am saying. A person who is taking care of the disabled loved one needs to have at least two times a week to get away for a few hours at a time. For example, I recommend an evening midweek when someone can take care of a loved one while the primary caretaker goes out to do something he or she enjoys. It used to amaze me when I heard people say they wouldn't know what to do for themselves. I hear that so much, and nowadays it seems to be the most common comment I get when I recommend this. Parents who have received a diagnosis for their child or family member almost without exception believe they can handle this situation forever. They do this because they love the one who needs the care. They do not understand the toll it takes over time. I encourage parents and families to apply for respite care when they first begin the process of care taking. I usually get resistance, but over time my experience has taught me that there comes a point when the parent and family recognize they need help. Hopefully, this will happen before burnout comes and despite how much you love a special needs person. Please believe me that in the majority of cases burnout will come.

There is another reason why I encourage families to apply for respite care and similar programs. Funding for these programs is no longer a priority as it has been in years past. Getting funded for respite care can take years, so the sooner a family applies the more likely they are to eventually benefit from these amazing programs. Some of these systems allow you to use family members or people you trust to become paid providers. Other programs may require you to use a licensed provider. How these programs are organized and administered will vary from state to state. Generally, you will be able to identify the licensed provider you desire by meeting with and discussing all your questions with potential providers. Please look into respite care programs in your state because I believe in the long run it will be in the best interest of you and your loved one.

Becoming a Respite Care Provider

If you want to become a provider for children or adults with special needs, there are opportunities to do so. Contact your state or local special needs programs by searching the internet using the words "special needs programs," "respite care," or even "foster care" and use your state, city, or county in the search criteria. There are a number of respite care programs looking for volunteers. If you would rather contribute in other ways besides becoming a direct provider of respite care, there are positions available for volunteer office staff or other ways to contribute. If you want to become a provider you may be looking at a considerable amount of training to learn respite care skills and possibly for foster care licensing. It depends on the area where you live and the policies governing these services.

Volunteer Respite Care Programs

There are many volunteer respite care programs and the majority are associated with colleges and universities. Because higher learning institutions require students to volunteer a certain number of hours, it makes this setting ideal for respite care. The model for most of these programs is similar in that families apply and, based on their needs, they are accepted. Depending on the different programs, parents are given two nights a month, give or take, to get away for a break from the care of their special needs child. Some programs will also take siblings. There is usually a nurse and a lead volunteer on duty during the day the respite is provided. The length of care is from two to four hours in most cases. Each child has his or her own folder with information regarding his or her needs and any special information for his or her safety. Each child will have at least one volunteer, and they are introduced to the parents before the parents leave the facility. Toileting and diaper changes are done with the nurse and volunteer present. Appropriate snacks are given, and the children and their volunteers are involved in activities as they are able to participate. The volunteers have background checks and are screened weekly on the national sex offender registry. The ages of the participants are from two to 18 years of age. If a family is receiving respite care services elsewhere, they are generally not able to qualify for these programs.

There is a website called ARCH or National Respite Network and Resource Center. http://archrespite.org. This is a remarkable place to learn more about respite care and to locate programs in your area, if they are available. There is another website called National Respite Guidelines, Building Principles for Respite Models and Services, which is www.lifespanrespite.memberlodge.org. It provides guidelines for establishing a respite program. I hope this information will assist people wherever there is no respite care to go forward and create such a program in their community.

chapter fifteen
SOME SUGGESTIONS WHEN THERE SEEMS TO BE LITTLE OR NO HELP

Helping Others When No Help Is Available

We have all been in a position to give comfort to those in need. Sometimes all we can be is a listening ear when there is no place to turn for help. The most frustrating moments in my job are when I have no idea where to direct someone. This is especially true if I am talking to a mother of a child who needs resources and I have to say, "I am not aware of any program that might be helpful for your needs." I always follow this up by saying, "That doesn't mean there might not be something out there that I am not aware of."

On the other hand, I feel a great deal of satisfaction when I am able to direct someone to a resource I believe he or she might benefit from. I also feel a special kind of satisfaction when I talk to someone who is angry because he or she has been getting nothing but the runaround. The funny thing is when I talk to these folks I oft times get all their anger. I have found if I just get past my automatic reaction of defensiveness and control my tendency to give back some of what they are giving me and just listen, we become friends. I have to take a deep breath and listen closely to what they are saying; over time, they invariably begin to drain off the pressure from their guilt, frustration, and helplessness. Afterward, they thank me for just allowing them to let it all out. This usually happens despite the fact I may not have helped in the least to resolve their problems. What I have learned to do is to become a listening ear, someone who does not talk or jump to conclusions. I just listen and make it safe for them to unload on me all the stuff that has been building, sometimes for years. I have felt a connection to each of these people, even if I never see or hear from them again. We become friends and, after much of the energy has dissipated, I will even voice some of my own frustrations with the system, lack of programs, funds, etc.

I recall one very vivid conversation with a woman who called my office many years ago. This mother had two daughters who had contracted a rare disease from something they ate at a restaurant. She had taken them to several specialists, and she did not believe they were getting the care they needed. She was feeling guilty, responsible, and helpless. Couple this with the frustration toward a number of doctors who seemed to be less than interested in her daughters. More bad news came with the endless stream of medical bills and doctors who would not return calls. She was intelligent, motivated and had done her research and homework, so she was ready with a barrage of questions, or you might describe it as an interrogation of any doctor she took her children to. Within a few minutes after the doctor entered the exam room, he would have felt like he had been ambushed by a formidable and knowledgeable mother who otherwise looked sweet and unassuming. I call these mothers "Storm Troopers," who hold everything in and let loose with all the energy they have built up over weeks and months of frustration. Don't get in their way; these are Mama Bears protecting their cubs.

I have had many of these conversations, and I am frequently surprised when, at the end of a 45 minute to an hour long conversation, (usually one sided) I end up liking the person who initially seemed angry, entitled, and disagreeable. I believe most of these parents are good people who have been pushed to the end of their proverbial rope because no one would listen or seemed to care. If you come across such a person, I hope you have the time to be the one who listens without comment and make a difference in his or her life. I believe you will be glad you did in the end.

When No Help Appears to Be Available What Do We Do?

You may be the person who is in need of a friend to talk to as in the above example. When you have been to your doctor or to other specialists and you seem to be stuck with nowhere to turn and very few answers to your problem, what can you do? Start by collecting your thoughts and feelings until you can get to a calm and resolved state. Do some relaxation exercises, or go for a walk. Do some talking to yourself or someone else, and, when you are in a better place mentally, start writing down all your questions and what you want to accomplish. Maybe you want a diagnosis for your child. Maybe you need help with finances to get the necessary treatment required. Write down your needs, whatever they are.

Here is the scary and possibly most difficult place to find yourself in: YOU may be the only answer. YOU MIGHT BE THE ONLY ONE WHO HAS THE DESIRE TO DO SOMETHING ABOUT THE LACK OF KNOWLEDGE, RESOURCES, TREATMENT, PROGRAMS, ETC. YOU MAY NEED TO START SOME KIND OF SUPPORT ORGANIZATION BECAUSE NOTHING ELSE EXISTS IN YOUR AREA.

You Can Be the Creator of Something Special to Help Not Only Yourself and Your Family but Many Others

Believe in yourself and your ability to make something happen. Contact those you know who may have similar concerns like the parents of other children at school, teachers, aides, and even people you run into at soccer games, stores, or doctor's offices who appear to have the same issues. Ask them if their needs are being met, and tell them your thoughts and concerns.

HOW DO YOU THINK ALL OF THE ORGANIZATIONS ACROSS THE WORLD BEGAN? THEY WERE STARTED

BY PEOPLE JUST LIKE YOU WHO HAD A CONCERN. YOU CAN DO THIS! BELIEVE IN YOURSELF AND MAKE SOMETHING GOOD HAPPEN.

I would love to see organizations spring up all over the planet to assist families who have special needs. It doesn't matter if you consider your need insignificant. You can bet there are many others out there who have family members with the same diagnosis or issues as yours, and they will be thinking just like you. They will also be thinking that their particular concerns are not very important. Don't let these feelings stop you from acting. Go out and talk with others and build a support system. You may be very surprised at the number of people who are in your boat.

Service to Others: The Key to Providing Help When No Help or Resources Are Available.

A woman who had two children with disabilities saw a need for recreation opportunities for not only her children but others as well. She contacted a local organization which helped disabled people to become more independent. They met and discussed her concerns, and that organization became the vehicle to notify others in the disabled community of her desire to create a program aimed at filling the need for recreational opportunities for disabled children. In a matter of a few months, a number of people came forward, mostly those who had children with disabilities who wanted to be involved. They put together an organization of volunteers who found facilities and the supervision necessary to provide several ongoing recreational activities for special needs children. Two positive outcomes resulted from this volunteer effort. First, the children were able to benefit from physical activity, enhanced social relationships, and simply having fun in activities, sports, and games. The second benefit was to give parents and siblings a break or respite from the ongoing care of the child during these activities. Parents and volunteers traded off conducting the various programs, giving the families of children with disabilities some downtime to spend on their own to rejuvenate themselves.

Suggestions When There Seems to be Little or No Help

You, as an individual, can make a big difference by acting on a simple idea and making it work. You have greater power than you think. I believe in the power of one person to make a difference. When you combine that power with even a few others who have the same vision, you can create something special.

In this day and age of limited programs and shrinking government budgets, we as a people need to start thinking about service and volunteerism in newer and more creative ways. I like the idea espoused by President George Herbert Walker Bush when he introduced the concept called "1000 Points of Light." The 1000 Points of Light referred to all the community organizations across the nation doing good things to help others. This organization began in 1990 and, after merging with another group, it is now called "Points of Light Institute." They have 200 local volunteer centers across the nation to connect volunteers with opportunities to serve. If there is such a center in your community or state, you may want to contact them and learn how to start a volunteer organization. If you already have something organized, Points of Light Institute may be able to help you with the names of volunteers who are ready to serve.

An excellent example of a volunteer organization is CHADD. This acronym stands for Children and Adults with Attention Deficit Disorder, their website is www.chadd.org. This is a nationwide organization of volunteers who labor in many areas to provide information on attention deficit disorder and attention deficit hyperactivity disorder. There may be some paid employees at the national organization level; however, local chapters are all volunteers. These are generally professionals or parents who have experience with patients or children and they want to help others. Local chapters volunteer their time to maintain web sites and other tasks like recruiting speakers for workshops and conventions. They do this at little or no cost to those who want to learn. These are highly motivated and caring people who can be a tremendous support to families. Ask questions and search the internet, and you may find an organization in your area that can help you and vice versa.

Craig T. Mitchell, LCSW

A Nonprofit Organization

Nonprofit organizations are established by businesses to help people and do not exist solely for the purpose of making money. They exist to have some kind of value to the public. They do not have stockholders who own a share of the company and then demand the organization make more profits so they can receive dividends. These organizations might be adoption agencies, counseling centers, and organizations that have and create programs for the good of people. Granted, there are many nonprofit companies who are in it for money, but laws keep this kind of organization in check for the most part. Nonprofit organizations have what are called boards of directors, who are in control of what the business does. They are made up of individuals in the community from all walks of life. They serve as board members with no financial compensation, except for reimbursement for travel expenses when they are required to travel long distances. In many instances these are remarkable people whose job it is to direct the organization for the greater good of the public. Some of these people spend many hours working within the organization to make sure all aspects of the work done are legally and ethically. Most of the agencies and organizations that help families are nonprofit and therefore qualify for lower tax rates than for profit businesses.

An example of a nonprofit organization would be an adoption agency that provides adoption services to birth parents, adoptive parents and who also may work with orphanages in foreign countries if they provide international adoptions. Another example might be an organization providing foster care services or women's shelters to house families who are in crisis. Some of these organizations help families with crisis nurseries, parenting classes, and other educational opportunities.

My point is that volunteer agencies, as well as nonprofit organizations, are generally where we are most likely to find helpful resources for our individual or family needs.

Learn About the Volunteer/Nonprofit Organizations in Your Community That Serve the Various Needs of Individuals and Families

Start asking questions of anyone who works with children with disabilities regarding either private organizations or publicly funded programs that might benefit your child. People you might ask include a parent who has a child with a disability, an early intervention worker, preschool worker, special education teachers, and program administrators. Health department nurses, staff, social workers, or therapists who provide occupational therapy, physical therapy, and speech therapy are also great resources. Your primary care physician, a hospital social worker, and even the receptionist at a local children's hospital (if you are fortunate to have one in your area) will all have information about special needs programs for children. You may want to ask for the social work department because in these settings social workers usually know about local resources.

START YOUR OWN ORGANIZATION

If You Can't Find an Organization to Fit Your Needs, Then Be the Answer for Yourself and Others and Start Your Own

This is exactly how most of these organizations and even businesses begin, with people just like you who are looking for help with a major concern. After much frustration and time spent on wild goose chases, the person or persons decide, "Let's get together and come up with information that will help not only us but others who will surely have the same needs."

In my community there exists a program that has been functioning for several years. It is an independent living center. It was created by parents who had children with disabilities that were soon becoming adults. They were concerned that their children would not have the resources to obtain everything from crutches to wheelchairs to wheelchair ramps in their homes. They also wanted to provide information about any resources that could be useful in helping young adults with disabilities be more self-sufficient. They contacted architects, draftsman, builders, contractors, and carpenters and asked if they would be willing to volunteer their time and expertise to assist individuals and families with disabilities. They were surprised to find many who were willing to participate. This program has grown to the extent that when a family or individual has a need for a wheelchair ramp, volunteers will go to the home and assess the situation. Plans are drawn up, material lists are prepared, and those willing to do the construction are identified. Sometimes donations are available to purchase materials, and when this is not possible the family saves until the funds are raised. They also have an impressive inventory of all kinds of what are called durable medical equipment such as wheelchairs, crutches, lifts, standers, beds, and other donated items they loan to those in need. Their office is always full of people with disabilities and others who are there to help, give advice, and who know how the systems within state, federal, and private programs operate.

There are all kinds of agencies established to help individuals and families which are funded by tax dollars and some private funds. Many are unknown to the general public. A significant number of individuals and families struggle along for years, without knowing there is help for them and their situations. These same processes can be applied to almost every need, if people are willing to move forward and take a leap of faith.

chapter sixteen
TRANSITION PLANNING FOR CHILDREN WITH SPECIAL NEEDS

There are two kinds of transition planning. One is for children who are in the Early Intervention program (for children from birth up to their third birthday). Before these children turn three they need to be transitioned into the Preschool Program if they continue to require services. The Preschool Program is for children ages three to five years who need therapies to hopefully reach their appropriate milestones before kindergarten. These milestones are described in the chapter entitled IDENTIFYING NORMAL AND DELAYED DEVELOPMENT IN CHILDREN.

Transition planning for teenagers is a process of planning the future for a child with special needs who is entering adulthood. This should be started between the ages of 14 to 16 or in some cases even earlier. Those involved in transition planning should be the parents, the school (generally meaning the special education department of the school), and other administration officials depending on school and state policy. There may be state agencies such as those who deal with people with disabilities and those who are responsible for rehabilitation services involved as well. Parents should inquire with the special education department of their child's school when the child is 14 years old regarding when transition planning should begin. Transition planning should be included in the child's IEP or Individualized Education Program.

Super Seniors

Some special needs children will remain in school until they are 22 years of age. This student is called a super senior. These individuals may not be able to pass competency tests in order to receive a high school diploma. They are retained in school and are in special education classes which they have probably been in most of their lives. They must have an IEP or Individualized Education Program in order to qualify for status as a super senior. This is part of Federal Legislation called the Americans with Disability Act of 1990. They are taught by special education teachers who are trained in special education methods and techniques. If the transition plan is done well, the future is laid out and available programs are applied to and put in place to provide the individual with structure and training programs, i.e. specialized schools, sheltered workshops, or other possibilities for special needs children as they enter adulthood. The types and availability of these programs depends on funding in your local area.

Independent Living Skills, ADLs or Activities of Daily Living

Independent living skills are also referred to as Activities of Daily Living or ADLs. These skills are taught by Special Education Teachers and Aides. They include learning how to ride public transportation, shopping skills using money and credit cards, house cleaning, laundry, and many other basic skills needed to help these students become as independent as possible. If you have a child with special needs and they have not learned these skills, you should talk to the special education department of your child's school and request a new Individualized Education Program to address these needs.

Guardianship

When a special needs child turns 18 and is not capable of living or functioning on his or her own, the parent or custodian of the child needs to apply for guardianship. In most places this must be done by an attorney because it has to be filed with the court, and there are technicalities requiring an attorney's expertise to make sure this is done correctly. The average cost in the state where I reside is about $1,000. It would be wise for parents to start saving for this necessary expense long before you get to this situation.

If you fail to do this, then when your child turns 18, you will have no legal rights to control what your child does in matters regarding finances, medical treatments, therapy, decisions regarding marriage, schooling, and every other aspect of his or her life. There are many heartbreaking stories I have heard over the years from parents who have not done this in a timely fashion. These vulnerable individuals have been taken advantage of, and their finances have been squandered while parents and family can legally do nothing to prevent it.

SSI and Medicaid

Supplemental Security Income is a program administered by the Social Security Administration for people with severe disabilities. It can provide the family with some financial assistance and, in the majority of cases, it will be an avenue for a child or adult who qualifies to receive Medicaid. To be eligible for SSI a person must qualify financially and medically. Financial qualifications take into account the number of children in the home besides the child who the family is applying for. They also consider earned family income, unearned income, child support, alimony, and the number of parents in the home. Medical eligibility is determined by a separate agency who requests medical records and other records from special programs and therapies the child is receiving. This process takes six months on average to complete. It is retroactive from the date one calls to apply so if the child qualifies the first check can be sizeable. The process is similar for adults applying for SSI. When a child turns 18 only his or her income is considered. Many who cannot qualify because of too much family income do qualify when they turn 18. In the majority of cases if a child receives SSI he or she will also qualify for Medicaid, but they must apply for Medicaid to receive it. Medicaid, simply put, is federal and state funded medical care.

Programs for People with Disabilities

As mentioned earlier, it would be well for you to check within your area to see if there are government departments with programs for people with disabilities. There may be training programs, sheltered workshops (a program that provides vocational and job skill training for special needs persons), group homes, or other programs that can provide special needs people with the ability to be as independent as possible.

Community Resources

The United Way in many areas publishes a Community Resource Directory. If you are looking for help with the concerns above, this is a good place to start your search. State departments for people with disabilities and rehabilitation services are good places to look. Universities are another excellent place to look for programs that list resources and provide community programs to evaluate children with special needs. Contact the child development, education, or social work departments of these institutions for such resources. The special education department of your local school district is also a good resource. Some school districts have parent resource centers, which house a host of material for special needs, learning disabilities, parenting assistance, and more. Internet searches for children with disabilities within your area may yield more local resources. State offices for individuals with disabilities are also good places to search. In closing, you may find some of your best help by talking to other parents who have children with special needs. Seek them out at your school's special education classes because many of these parents are experts at finding and utilizing programs. Good luck!

chapter seventeen
MEDICAL PROVIDERS AND INSURANCE COMPANIES

A medical or health care provider can be a doctor, physician's assistant, nurse practitioner, or any other professional who works in the health care field. Pediatric specialists are different than other doctors because they treat only children up to the ages of 18 to 21. With regard to children with special needs some pediatricians may see these patients until they are the age of 23 if the child is still in public school. Some of these special children are called Super Seniors because they are allowed to stay in public school until they turn 23. They are usually in special education classes, and staying in school as a Super Senior can be very advantageous providing much more training in areas of what are called Activities of Daily Living or ADLs. These skills make individuals with disabilities as independent as possible.

What kind of Medical Provider Do I Need for My child?

Pediatricians are typically the best, although there are many family practice doctors, physician's assistants, or nurse midwives who do an excellent job of treating children.

One note here to caution you, some medical practices are owned by high pressure business groups who require all providers from doctors, physician's assistants, and nurse midwives to see a very large number of patients per day. In these situations, it is important to understand that you may get a precious few minutes with your medical provider because he or she is constantly trying to keep up with a quota each day. It may seem like they don't care or aren't listening to you when it might be their situation rather than their bedside manner.

Primary Care Physicians or PCPs

In this day and age your doctor is also called the Primary Care Physician or PCP. This is important to know because he or she is also called the gate keeper, meaning they serve as the point person who decides what kind of treatment or type of medical specialist you are allowed to see. With some insurance companies this is a hard, fast rule that no one can avoid because if you don't see the PCP first the insurance company may not pay for the exam/evaluation with a specialist. Your PCP may not actually be a doctor; it might be a Physician's Assistant, Nurse Practitioner, or Nurse Midwife.

(Special Note: With the Affordable Care Act, the type of treatment we receive may be taken out the hands of our medical provider and placed into the domain of government policies, programs, and employees. It may take some time for the changes to become understood by the general public. Much of the information in this chapter was written prior to this new law taking effect, however many aspects will remain the same.)

Health Maintenance Organizations (HMOs) and Preferred Provider Organizations (PPOs)

Some health insurance companies are called HMOs or a Health Maintenance Organization which may be a hospital system. Some of these HMO corporations are huge and own many hospitals, clinics, and medical facilities, and have almost every kind of specialist one might need. In these cases, you generally need a referral from your Primary Care Physician to a medical specialist because the HMO employs their own providers, or they contract with providers to see their clients for a set fee. HMOs are highly controlling of who you can see outside the list of their own employees/providers. They will not allow you to go to a provider outside their network of providers unless it is an emergency. Insurance companies may contract with HMOs or individual hospitals, clinics, doctors, labs, medical providers, etc. to provide services for their packaged programs, which, in turn, they sell to businesses and government agencies, etc. If an insurance company contracts with individual hospitals and medical providers, they will have a list of these providers you will be able to see as a patient and you will have a copay.

PPOs or Preferred Provider Organizations allow you more choices to see the providers you want to see; however, you will most likely pay more for your copays and deductibles. You will pay less if you chose a provider within the PPO's network.

I have been amused over the years to hear all kinds of people from politicians to news agencies to individuals who complain about the lack of coverage people receive from their health insurance company. This way of thinking is somewhat backwards because each HMO or Health Insurance Company has all kinds of plans they sell to companies and government agencies from very basic benefits with few options for treatment to excellent coverage providing a wide range of medical services. The company who purchases the health care product from the insurance company determines what program they want to pay for, and their employees are stuck with what they purchase. Therefore, when someone is unhappy with their health coverage, they should blame their employer not the insurance company for what they don't cover. To blame the insurance companies for not providing certain treatment options is like an employee who is upset with a car manufacturer for not providing the same options on their company's cars as their competitor provides for their company cars. Each company is a business that buys certain kinds of cars based on choices made from budgets by the executives in charge. If they are concerned about the comfort of their employees and are doing well financially they might decide to purchase bigger, more expensive vehicles with more options. Others, not so well off, will purchase the small economy cars with no air conditioning, power locks, etc. When the purchase is made the employees have to live with what is purchased. The same concept exists with health insurance. An employer buys a specific health care package, and the employee has no other option.

I used to work for a large health insurance company who contracted with mental health facilities to provide treatment for drug and alcohol as well as psychiatric treatment. They sold their health care packages to large companies. Some plans were very generous to their employees and some were very basic in their coverage. These plans had two forms of coverage. Medical health care included hospitalization, outpatient services, primary care doctors' visits and possibly dental and optical. The second area covered mental health. My job was to authorize patient stays in different mental health hospital settings. These stays included treatment for drug and alcohol abuse; the maximum was 30 days. Other psychiatric treatment was also included with certain limits that could not be extended beyond the contracted amount.

We had contracts with huge companies who bought certain mental health coverages for their employees. We had huge policy books indicating exactly what the coverage was for each company or employer. We could not authorize any treatment outside the contracted agreement made with that company. I received many threatening phone calls from angry employees who wanted their family member to stay in a treatment center for longer than the contract allowed. There was nothing I could do. The companies who purchased the mental health product hid behind the insurance company, all the while knowing the policies they paid for would not provide certain treatments. All I could do was to tell the frustrated employee what the policy covered and that I could not authorize any stays longer than what the policies stated. Sometimes the company/employer would step in and pay for longer stays if they were benevolent enough. This happened on a number of occasions. As I recall, when this happened an employee would generally have go to his or her supervisor and the supervisor would appeal to the company and sometimes they would pay for the extra care needed from company funds. If you run into such a situation you may want to go to your supervisor or your Human Resources Office and request if the company would be willing to fund a certain treatment for you or your family member, if it is not covered in your policy. Your employer's Human Resources Office would know if such arrangements might be possible.

Very sadly, some insurance companies avoid providing mental health care benefits. Hopefully the Affordable Care Act will change this. I have been a provider for a number of companies who contract with businesses or insurance companies to provide these benefits. They identify and contract with counselors and therapists in their coverage areas and refer patients to them when they receive calls from employees. Some of these programs are called Employee Assistance Programs or EAP.

I discuss EAP programs in other chapters. Many of these programs are excellent and provide a valuable service to their employees and their families.

chapter eighteen
CHOOSING A PRIMARY CARE PHYSICIAN OR MEDICAL PROVIDER

If you, as a parent, have a concern regarding your child then make an appointment with your child's medical provider and go in with a list of questions prepared ahead of time. Depending on several factors, you may find good or even very poor results when asking questions regarding your child. This may be due to a number of factors, so let's review them now. You may have a provider who has an excellent bedside manner and takes interest in his or her patients. On the other hand, you may have a provider who has very poor listening skills and may be either mildly helpful or just downright rude and insensitive. We have all seen or heard of doctors who have an attitude that they are just putting up with you and you leave the office feeling like you have been put in your place as a second-class citizen. This may be the doctor and his or her personality, or it may be the result of who he or she works for.

Doctor's Offices as Business Offices

There is a recent phenomenon which is now part of our world, and that phenomenon is that many doctor's offices are owned and operated by high-pressure corporations. These kinds of businesses require their providers to meet a quota of ridiculous numbers of patients per day. This creates a conveyor belt type mentality on behalf of the provider, leaving little or no time to respond to very real concerns or even simple questions from the patient or caregivers. Most of the time, these medical practices are owned by a corporation that has nothing to do with medicine and has purchased the practice in order to make money. I have seen a number of doctors who have left practices because of this business type of medicine, causing high stress and unfulfilling practices for the doctor and patients. This puts the public at risk because best practices are sometimes relegated to second place behind reaching the quota for the day. I don't believe doctors are in favor of this kind of work environment; they are just placed in a very difficult position to provide numbers over patient care. Their jobs are literally at stake in these situations. You may want to inquire regarding these matters when you are searching for a provider for your child or anyone in the family for that matter. Just being aware of the possibility of this situation existing may make a difference in who you choose for a health care provider. Shopping for a good provider is at least as important as shopping for a good plumber, contractor, or for good quality products that will stand the test of time. You are putting your family's health and lives on the line here, and you do not have to settle for someone who does not meet your expectations.

Searching for a Primary Care Physician

The first thing you need to do is to ask people who live in your area regarding who they use as their medical provider. Word-of-mouth is the best way to find good providers because of trust based on positive experiences. There are now ratings for medical providers online so you might want to do a search and see what you can find about individual providers. You will probably be limited to the providers on your health insurance provider list.

Your Insurance Company May Have a List of Providers You Must Choose From

If you have insurance the number of providers you are allowed to see may be small or large depending on the kind of policy you have. You will need to obtain a list of medical providers from your insurance company called "Preferred Providers." This list will typically be the only providers your insurance company will allow you to use. If you do not want to use them, or let's say in an emergency you go to someone else not on the list, you will be going to a provider who is called "Out of Network." In many cases insurance companies will not pay for a provider who is out of network (or they may pay a minimal amount). Therefore, you may be responsible to pay for any provider you use who is not on your insurance company's provider list. You should also check to see what your co pay is for a preferred provider. You can do so by contacting your insurance provider.

Be Aware!

Based on new laws coming into effect in the future, it is unclear how all this current information will be impacted. It will be important to write down and ask every question you have regarding possible providers and what financial responsibility you have for each one before making any appointment.

Physician's Assistants and Nurse Practitioners

You have probably noticed that many medical clinics today have Physician's Assistants (PA) and/or Nurse Practitioners (NP). Many of these providers are very competent and practice under the supervision of a medical doctor in treating everything from aches and pains to infectious diseases to everyday illnesses we encounter such as colds, flu, sprains, etc. If a PA or NP is unsure about symptoms or a diagnosis, he or she can consult with one of the doctors in the practice. Many medical specialists now have Physician's Assistants and Nurse Practitioners on staff.

My wife and I took our children to a pediatrician who has been a close family friend for many years. He has always been in such demand that at times we could not get an appointment with him, especially if we had a child with an acute illness needing treatment right away. When we could not get in to see him, we asked for a specific Physician's Assistant because we found him to be very competent, and it was easy to get an appointment with him. On a few occasions he would consult with the doctor. I work next to a clinic that has Nurse Practitioners and Physician's Assistants, and I go to see them when I become ill. I am very comfortable with these providers, and if you choose to see one, I hope you are able to find someone in whom you have confidence.

Nurse Midwives

Nurse Midwives provide prenatal care and delivery for pregnant women. If they have their own private practices, they must have a medical doctor on call at all times in case their patients require cesarean sections or some other form of surgery. This may vary according to the state or country where you live. You should also be aware that in quite a few practices when you make an appointment you might think you will be seeing a doctor when, in fact, you might be scheduled with a Nurse Practitioner or Physician's Assistant. As mentioned, many of these people are excellent providers, and you might find that they are easier to get appointments with, and they frequently spend more time with their patients than do doctors. They are generally very good for treating colds, flu, sore throats, and all kinds of other common ailments. Some practices such as Ear, Nose and Throat and many other specialists use these professionals to diagnose and treat patients. If given a chance, you may be very happy with their performance.

Disclaimer: Word of Caution, just as in all fields of medicine and in life, you may come across providers, be they doctors, PA's, NP's, or Midwives who range from excellent to very poor. Be wise and ask all the questions you can think of as you chose a provider.

If You Have Insurance

If you have insurance, you may be restricted to certain hospitals, clinics, or providers which could be further away from your home and make your search more difficult. It can also make travel to appointments inconvenient. If you have a family member with a special need you will probably be even more restricted because specialists may be found at only one hospital or clinic.

Out of Network

As already stated, choosing a hospital or any type of medical provider outside of your insurance's list of acceptable providers is called "Out of Network." This makes everyone cringe when they hear this statement from their insurance company. This means that the insurance provider may not pay anything toward treatment or only a percentage of what is called "Customary Fees."

There are a number of reasons why someone would choose to use an out of network medical provider. One instance might be if you have a child who has a condition you believe should only be treated by pediatric specialists at a specific children's hospital and your insurance does not contract with that hospital. You may choose to use the children's hospital and their doctors. Your insurance company will have policies in place about these kinds of situations. Check them out prior to scheduling an appointment with any provider or hospital. Sometimes special arrangements can be made with your insurance company or your employer to make this happen. This will, in most cases, only be possible if you work for a large employer who is willing to work with or even beyond what the insurance company will pay. In these cases, you need to contact the human resources office where you or your spouse are employed. You might be able to get an exception or a percentage of the bill paid. It is worth a try.

At this time the new healthcare bill is not fully functioning, and it could change access to make available more providers than are currently on your insurance company's network lists. Upcoming changes in health care policy will make navigating these policies more complicated as the medical world changes faster than average users can adapt.

If You Don't Have Insurance or Will Be Using an Out of Network Provider or Hospital

If you don't have insurance and you will be paying out of pocket, then you need to know which providers, clinics, or hospitals will work with you in terms of making payments. You will want to know if they charge interest and how much the interest is. If you can go into a doctor or hospital with cash you can generally get a much better break in fees by paying up front.

Don't Get Caught Paying for a Doctor Who is Out of Network; Check in Advance Before Getting Surgery or a Procedure Done

An excellent example of being stuck with an out of network provider, in my personal experience, is with Anesthesiologists. On several occasions when my family members have required surgery they also needed an anesthesiologist. These doctors are responsible to put patients to sleep or administer medications to numb pain during surgery and other procedures. In my area, many of these doctors are not associated with hospitals and have formed medical groups. This being the case, you need to know which anesthesiologist group or individual doctor is covered by your insurance program prior to having a procedure done. Sometimes this is difficult to do because the hospital or facility does not know which doctor will be there on any given day. I have had to pay extra out of pocket fees for several of these doctors because they were not on my insurance's provider list. You should have little, if any problem, making sure your surgeon is on your provider list. However, just because you are going to a hospital or same-day surgery center covered by your insurance carrier, does not mean that all doctors or providers who are working there will be covered. Ask questions and be diligent. You may have to get a little assertive to find out about these details. With these matters "An ounce of prevention is worth a pound of cure."

Is He or She a Family Practice, or General Practice Provider?

A family practice provider or a general practice provider is someone who usually treats all family members from infants to older patients.

Do They Have Any Age Restrictions?

Some of these providers may have age restrictions regarding who they will treat. Therefore, you need to ask if they see patients from birth to death, if that is what your family needs. There are specialists who treat senior citizens, and they are called Gerontologists. If you have an older family member who needs help from someone who really understands what they need then ask your doctor or other health care professionals for referrals to a Gerontologist.

Many clinics now days have several specialists who can provide almost all of what a family requires. If you are fortunate you may have one clinic which meets all your family's medical needs. If your family is young and you will be having children you may want to ask, "Do you provide obstetrics?" (Which is the care of women during pregnancy, childbirth and after childbirth). Do they provide pediatric care would be the next question to ask since this involves following children from birth into adulthood. You will also want to know when your child is born if the doctor will visit him or her at the hospital.

Often some medical providers in outlying areas and small communities where an obstetrician is not available, will provide obstetrics and even follow patients through their entire life cycle.

Do You Perform Circumcisions, If This Is Something You Want Done?

Another question you may want to ask if you are going to give birth and are considering a family practice or general practitioner concerns circumcision, if you want this done. Family practice or general practitioners may or may not do this, and you need to know. In smaller communities these types of providers will usually perform this procedure.

If You are Female and You Need Gynecology for Ongoing Female Care

Gynecologists are doctors who take care of women's needs from pap smears which can detect uterine and ovarian cancer to breast exams and treatment of hormonal imbalances. They also help with issues involving menopause. They can also treat disorders of the female reproductive organs. Ask if they provide gynecology services.

OB/GYN's

Doctors who provide obstetrics (prenatal care and birth and delivery of babies) and gynecology are called OB/GYN's. There are many women who use these doctors as their primary care physician.

chapter nineteen
MEDICAL SPECIALISTS LIST AND DEFINITIONS

Medical Specialists List and Definitions

This is not a complete list of all specialists, but I am citing many of the more common ones of which you should be aware.

The Difference Between Pediatric and Adult Specialists

There are specialists, called pediatric specialists, who treat only children. They may see patients up to the age of 18 to 21. Adult specialists will generally see patients from 18 to senior citizens. There are some exceptions to this, based on the type of doctor and practice. If you have younger children, you may prefer to see pediatric providers because they are used to dealing with infants and children. Hopefully, they will be a little more patient and understanding with small children who may be reactive to being examined.

Allergist or Immunologist

This is a medical doctor who diagnoses and treats problems related to allergies such as hay fever, asthma, skin rashes, and other physical reactions to everything from pollen to bug bites and reactions to all kinds of substances.

Cardiologist

This is a medical doctor who diagnoses and treats heart disease. Some cardiologists obtain further training to become cardiac surgeons, who operate on the heart.

Dentist/Orthodontist

A dentist has gone to dental school and diagnoses and treats teeth. A dentist may also go on for further training to become an orthodontist. An orthodontist specializes in straightening teeth with the use of braces and many newer technologies. They can align teeth and jaw problems for most people at any age. They prefer to see patients by the age of seven years.

Dermatologist

This is a doctor who diagnoses and treats problems of the skin.

Endocrinologist

This is a doctor who diagnoses diseases of the glands such as thyroid disease, diabetes, hormones, menopause, hypertension (high blood pressure), osteoporosis, cholesterol and other related diseases.

Gastroenterologist (sometimes referred to as GI doctors)

These are doctors who treat the diseases of the digestive system. This includes from the mouth, to the throat, stomach, and bowels. Common diagnoses they treat include heartburn, acid reflux, stomach ulcers, and diseases of the intestines and colon.

Hematologist/Oncologist

These are doctors who deal with the diagnosis and treatment of diseases of the blood such as sickle cell anemia. They can also generally treat cancer of the blood called leukemia and lymphoma.

Hospitalist

This is a doctor who is located at a hospital and can admit, diagnose, and treat a patient if the primary care physician is not available.

Infectious Disease Doctors

These doctors diagnose and treat rare diseases like hepatitis, Lyme disease, and many other less common diseases.

Geneticist

These doctors try to identify and treat the causes of the many types of birth defects and genetic disorders which can be caused by our heredity or genes.

Geriatrics

This is a doctor who takes care of elderly people.

Neonatologist

These doctors treat newborn children who are premature at birth or who have various medical problems that put them at risk. Many infants are able to survive very difficult circumstances at birth because of the efforts of these professionals and hospital staff.

Nephrologist

This is a doctor who diagnoses and treats diseases of the kidneys like diabetes. They deal with many of the same problems as do Urologists but they do not generally perform surgery. They are concerned with how the kidneys function.

Neurologist

A doctor who diagnoses and treats brain disorders like seizures or strokes. They prescribe antiseizure medications and order EEGs (Electroencephalograms) to detect seizure disorders. Sometimes an MRI or other tests are needed.

Neurosurgeon

This is a doctor who performs surgery on the brain.

Obstetrician/Gynecologist

An Obstetrician provides prenatal care for women who are pregnant or are in need of birth control or reproductive health. They deliver babies and perform cesarean sections when the baby is at risk during delivery. Most Obstetricians are also Gynecologists who treat women as they transition into menopause and perform pap smear tests as well as help with hormone replacement therapy, if needed. They are often called OB/GYNs. Some of these doctors also specialize in diagnosing and treating couples who have infertility (inability to become pregnant or to carry a fetus to full-term and have a successful delivery).

Oncologist

Oncology is the study of tumors and cancers, so a doctor who diagnoses and treats cancer is an Oncologist. Depending on the type of cancer one has, the diagnosis will determine what kind of Oncologist he or she will need to see. If the patient is a child he or she will probably be treated by a Hematologist/Oncologist. With adult patients it is becoming more specialized to the point where some Oncologists only treat one specific kind of cancer such as breast cancer, ovarian cancer, or lung cancer. This is when a primary care physician becomes very important to refer their patients to the appropriate type of Oncologist they will need for proper treatment.

Radiation Oncologist

This is a doctor who treats tumors and cancer with radiation.

Ophthalmologist

This is a doctor who diagnoses and treats diseases of the eye. Many Ophthalmologists do surgeries as well, such as cataract removal or corneal transplants.

Optometrist

This is a doctor who does eye exams and can diagnose and treat certain eye diseases not requiring surgery. These are the doctors who give eye exams at offices where you go to get your eye glasses or contacts. They are found in many of the retail stores who have optical departments.

Oral Maxillofacial/Oral Surgeon

These doctors diagnose and treat diseases and injuries to the mouth or jaw. Examples include removal of wisdom teeth, cleft lip and palate, and repairing injuries to the face and jaw.

Orthopedic Surgeon or Orthopod

These are doctors who diagnose and treat problems of the bones and muscles. These doctors see children and adults who have cerebral palsy and other disorders which require braces and treatments to help with muscles which are too tight or too loose. They prescribe braces, physical therapy, occupational therapy, and they also perform surgery to replace hips and knees, as well as repairing damage to knees and other joints. Pediatric orthopedic surgeons are very helpful in treating children with disabilities who require crutches, braces, or wheelchairs. These are the doctors who prescribe wheelchairs, standers, lifts, and other equipment to assist children with orthopedic concerns.

Otolaryngologists

These doctors are commonly referred to as ENTs or ear, nose, and throat specialists. They diagnose and treat diseases of the ear, nose, and throat. They often also do surgeries to remove tonsils, adenoids, and to place PE tubes in ears for children who have chronic (long-term) ear infections.

Pathologists

These doctors try to determine the causes, processes and effects of disease, including many diseases which are rare and hard to diagnose.

Pediatrician

A Pediatrician is a doctor who treats only children up to the age of either 18 or 21 depending on the doctor's preference.

Physical Medicine, Rehabilitation Physicians or Physiatrists

These doctors work with patients in rehabilitation hospitals or similar settings with patients who have disabilities or have had accidents, strokes, etc. They direct the patient's various therapies such as speech, occupational (fine motor or small muscle groups, such as writing skills), and physical therapy (gross motor or large muscle groups, such as sitting, standing, and walking). These doctors also give Botox and phenol injections into muscles for patients who have high muscle tone and require help in relaxing these tight muscles which are referred to as contractures.

Plastic Surgeon

This is a doctor who repairs various areas of the body usually with transfer of tissue (grafts) and other methods. With infants, plastic surgeons repair cleft lips and palates and other deformities related to birth defects.

Pulmonologist

This is a doctor specializing in the lungs and breathing. People who have asthma, emphysema, or tuberculosis would be treated by this type of specialist.

Radiologist

This is a professional who may be a technician or a doctor. They diagnose and treat medical problems using various imaging techniques such as CT scans and MRIs.

Rheumatologist

These are doctors who diagnose and treat diseases of the joints, bones, and muscles. This includes arthritis, osteoporosis, lupus, gout, and fibromyalgia.

General Surgeon

This is a surgeon who normally operates on the abdomen and the organs involved in that area of the body. They repair hernias or perform appendectomies and many other kinds of general surgeries.

Pediatric Surgeon

These doctors diagnose and operate on many kinds of conditions in children. When they treat patients from the fetus in the womb, it is called prenatal surgery. They also treat newborn infants, who are referred to as neonatal infants as well as older children.

Thoracic Surgeon

These are surgeons who operate on the heart, lungs, and other organs in the chest. Included in the designation of thoracic surgeons are various cardiac surgeons as well.

Urologist

This is a doctor who deals with the urinary tract, involving the kidneys, bladder, and male reproductive organs including erectile dysfunction, which is called impotence. Most of these doctors perform surgery. They treat patients with kidney stones and male infertility problems.

Now you will be more educated when and if you need a specific doctor or provider.

NAVIGATING LIFE
When and How to Involve a Professional

Book 1
In this book, you will discover what therapy is and how it helps heal anxiety, depression, PTSD, abuse and other mental, emotional problems. You will learn the difference between psychiatrists, psychologists and counselors and how medication works for mental health treatment. When you understand how counseling is done you will be more comfortable using the included suggestions for finding a counselor.

Book 2
In this book, you will learn about adoption, ADHD, autism, developmental delays in children and how to identify them, special needs, respite care and how to find special medical providers and primary care doctors. You will understand how to help your child using IEPs and 504 Accommodations and where to turn for support.

Book 3
In this book, you will learn about understanding personalities, fears, what to do prior to marriage, how to keep marriage working, the damage divorce causes, costs of going to counseling, why people don't go to counseling, what happens if they go or don't go, what marriage counseling is like, getting help in domestic abuse and the basics of parenting.

About the Author

With a degree in Psychology and Master's of Social Work, Craig has been practicing for 40 years in psychotherapy, marriage and family counseling. He has treated patients with varying mental/emotional disorders, including victims of sexual abuse. He was a foster parent for children with special needs and assisted parents who have children with special needs. He has worked with domestic and international adoptions for his entire career. He is the father of 7 children and 12 grandchildren. He loves being with his family and once this book is finished, he can't wait to get to the golf course.

Made in the USA
Las Vegas, NV
06 October 2021